The Cunning of History

The Holocaust and the
American Future

RICHARD L. RUBENSTEIN

HARPER COLOPHON BOOKS
Harper & Row, Publishers
New York, Hagerstown, San Francisco, London

To Charles E. Merrill, Jr.
in appreciation of two decades
of friendship

A hardcover edition of this book is published by Harper & Row, Publishers.

THE CUNNING OF HISTORY. Copyright © 1975 by Richard L. Rubenstein. Introduction copyright © 1978 by William Styron. All rights reserved. Printed in the United States of America. No part of this book may be used or reproduced in any manner without written permission except in the case of brief quotations embodied in critical articles and reviews. For information address Harper & Row, Publishers, Inc., 10 East 53d Street, New York, N.Y. 10022. Published simultaneously in Canada by Fitzhenry & Whiteside Limited, Toronto.

First edition published 1975

First HARPER COLOPHON edition, with new Introduction, published 1978

ISBN: 0–06–090597–2

81 82 10 9 8 7 6 5

Contents

Foreword

I wish to express my appreciation to Mr. Clayton Carlson, Ms. Marie Cantlon, and the staff of Harper & Row for their help in editing and producing this book. I am especially indebted to Mr. Carlson for encouraging me to write a book on "current issues in American society and politics." I am also indebted to Professor Herbert Richardson of St Michael's College, the University of Toronto, for his counsel in determining the final shape this work has taken. I would also like to thank my colleagues at Florida State University, especially Professor Lawrence Cunningham and Dr. Neil Hurley, S.J., for their helpful assistance. My research associate, Mrs. Betty Phifer, was, as usual, of great help and encouragement as was Professor John Carey, Chairman of the Department of Religion at Florida State University. My students gave me the opportunity to test out some of my ideas both before and after they were committed to paper. I am grateful to the Graduate Research Council of Florida State University and the Rockefeller Foundation for the support they have given to the Center for the Study of Southern Culture and Religion. A number of the insights expressed in this book were developed as a result of research I had done in my capacity as director of the Center. Dean William Hamilton of Portland State University, Portland, Oregon, read part of my manuscript and made helpful suggestions. My thanks also go to my friend of many years, Henry Koerner of Pittsburgh, Pennsylvania and Vienna, Austria, one of the truly great artists of our time. I shall never forget the hours I spent in the restaurants and coffee houses of Vienna in August, 1974 sharing the contents of this book with him. Ms. Julianna Klein of Tallahassee was extremely helpful in the typing of the manuscript.

Above all, my thanks go to my wife, Betty Rogers Rubenstein, who gave me her daily encouragement and offered her wise and helpful criticism of the entire manuscript.

Valladolid
Madrid
Florence
Summer 1974

Introduction

William Styron

Few books possess the power to leave the reader with that feeling of awareness that we call a sense of revelation. *The Cunning of History* seems to me to be one of these. It is a very brief work—a long essay—but it is so rich in perception and it contains so many startling—indeed, prophetic—insights that one can only remain baffled at the almost complete absence of attention it suffered when it was first published in 1975. When I first read Rubenstein's book I felt very much the same effect of keen illumination that I did when, in the early stages of writing *The Confessions of Nat Turner*, I happened to read Stanley Elkins's *Slavery*—a work that shed fresh light on American Negro slavery in such a bold and arresting way that, despite the controversy it provoked and the revisionist criticism it produced, it has become a classic in its field. It is perhaps a fitting coincidence that Rubenstein discusses Elkins at some length in this book; certainly both writers share a preoccupation with what to my mind is perhaps the most compelling theme in history, including the history of our own time—that of the catastrophic propensity on the part of human beings to attempt to dominate one another.

If slavery was the great historical nightmare of the eighteenth and nineteenth centuries in the Western world, it was slavery's continuation, in the horror we have come to call Auschwitz, which is the nightmare of our own century. Auschwitz, like the core of hell, is the symbolic center of *The Cunning of History,* and while the theological and political ramifications radiating from this center provide many of the book's most illuminating insights, it is Auschwitz—simply Auschwitz—that remains Rubenstein's primary concern. We are still very close to Auschwitz in time; its unspeakable monstrousness—one is tempted to say its unbelievability—continues to leave us weak with trauma, haunting us as with the knowledge of some lacerating bereavement. Even as it recedes slowly into the past it taxes our belief, making us wonder if it really happened. As a concept, as an image, we shrink from it as from damnation itself. "Christmas and Easter can be subjects for poetry," wrote W. H. Auden, "but Good Friday, like Auschwitz, cannot. The reality is so horrible. . . ." To this he might have added the near impossibility not just of poetry but of prose, even of an expository sort. The critic George Steiner has suggested the ultimate response: silence. But of course writers cannot be silent, least of all a questing writer like Rubenstein, who has set himself the admirable but painful task of anatomizing the reality within the nightmare while the dream is still fresh.

As near in time as Auschwitz is to us, it is nonetheless an historical event, and one of the excellences of Rubenstein's book is the audacious and original way in which the author has confronted the event, wringing from its seeming incomprehensibility the most subtle and resonant meanings. This is an unusual achievement when one considers how frequently analyses of the historical process become little more than tendentious exercises reflecting the writer's bias, which in turn corresponds to the pieties of the era in which he writes. So often the product is less history than wish-fulfillment, reinforcing the prejudices of his contemporaries and their hearts' desire. A brief word about the incredibly dramatic shift in attitudes in the writing of the history of American Negro slavery may serve to illustrate this. During the roughly three quarters of a century between the Emancipation Proclamation and the Second World War, the historiography of slavery generally reflected the mood of a society that remained profoundly racist, committed to the notion of racial inferiority and to the unshakable virtues of segregation. Towering above all other historians of slavery in the decades before the war was the Georgia-born scholar Ulrich B. Phillips whose work, despite certain undoubted merits of scholarship, was heavily weighted in favor of the portrayal of slave times as an almost Elysian period, in which contented slave and indulgent master were united in an atmosphere of unexacting, productive labor and domestic tranquillity.

By the 1940s, however, the winds of change were blowing; the social upheavals of the preceding decade had drastically affected the national consciousness, bringing with them a perception of the outrages and injustices still being perpetrated on the Negro. Also, a certain sophistication had evolved regarding the psychology of suffering. It would thus seem inevitable, in this new atmosphere of nagging guilt and self-searching, that the writing of the history of slavery would undergo drastic revisionism, and it was just as likely that the new portrait of antebellum times would be the very antithesis of Ulrich B. Phillips's softly tinted idyll; most of the new scholarship (epitomized by Kenneth B. Stampp's *The Peculiar Institution*) represented slavery as unremittingly harsh, cruel, and degrading, with few if any redeeming aspects. It was one of the great virtues of Elkins's *Slavery*, coming a few years later (and, as I say, its catalytic power in terms of its subject seems to me similar to that of Rubenstein's present work), that it struck violently through the obfuscations and preconceptions that had dictated, often self-righteously, the views of the apologists for slavery on the one hand, and its adversaries on the other, and, in effect, demanded that the institution be examined from any number of new and different angles objectively, in all of its difficult complexity. Aspects of Elkins's own thesis, which are not truly relevant here, have undergone severe criticism, but his insights have been gratefully absorbed into the remarkable body of scholarship that has grown around the subject of American slavery in the last twenty years and that has perhaps been most richly realized in the work of Eugene D. Genovese.

There was of course really nothing defensible about slavery. But unlike slavery—which, after all, has had its quixotic defenders—Auschwitz can have no proponents whatever. Therefore I am not suggesting that in *The Cunning of History* Rubenstein is acting as an intermediary in a debate or is synthesizing opposing points of view. What I am saying is that, like Elkins, Rubenstein is forcing us to reinterpret the meaning of Auschwitz—especially, although not exclusively, from the standpoint of its existence as part of a continuum of slavery that has been engrafted for centuries onto the very body of Western civilization. Therefore, in the process of destroying the myth and the preconception, he is making us see that that encampment of death and suffering may have been more horrible than we had ever imagined. It was slavery in its ultimate embodiment. He is making us understand that the etiology of Auschwitz—to some a diabolical, perhaps freakish excrescence, which vanished from

the face of the earth with the destruction of the crematoria in 1945—
is actually embedded deeply in a cultural tradition that stretches back
to the Middle Passage from the coast of Africa, and beyond, to the
enforced servitude in ancient Greece and Rome.

Rubenstein is saying that we ignore this linkage, and the existence of
the sleeping virus in the bloodstream of civilization, at risk of our future.

If it took a hundred years for American slavery to become demyth-
ified, one can only wonder when we can create a clear understanding of
Auschwitz, despite its proximity to us in time. For several years now I
have been writing a work—part fiction, part factual—which deals to a
great extent with Auschwitz and I have been constantly surprised at the
misconceptions I have encountered with enlightened people whenever
the subject has come up in conversation. The most common view is that
the camp was a place where Jews were exterminated by the millions in
gas chambers—simply this and nothing more. Now it is true that in their
genocidal fury the Nazis had consecrated their energies to the slaughter
of Jews en masse, not only at Auschwitz, where two and a half million
Jews died, but at such other Polish extermination centers as Belzec,
Treblinka, Majdanek, and Chelmno. And of course countless victims
died at camps in Germany. In 1943, a directive from the *Reichsführer
SS*, Heinrich Himmler, plainly stated that all European Jews would be
murdered without exception, and we know how close to success the
execution of that order came.

But at Auschwitz—the supreme example of that world of "total
domination" that Rubenstein sees as the arch-creation of the Nazi
genius—there was ultimately systematized not only mass murder on a
scale never known before, but also mass slavery on a level of bestial
cruelty. This was a form of bondage in which the victim was forced to
work for a carefully calculated period (usually no more than three
months) and then, through methods of deprivation calculated with
equal care, allowed to die. As Rubenstein points out, only in a situation
where human bodies were endlessly replaceable could such a form of
slavery prove to be efficient—but the Nazis, who were this century's
original efficiency experts, had no cause for concern on this count,
supplied as they were with all the Jews of Europe, besides thousands of
Poles, Russian prisoners of war, and others. These became victims of a
bureaucratic *modernization* of slavery. And although the concept was

not entirely unique in the long chronicle of bondage (for a period in the West Indies the British, with a glut of manpower, had no qualms about working slaves to death) certainly no slaveholders had on such a scale and with such absolute ruthlessness utilized human life in terms of its simple *expendability*. Rubenstein explains in his persuasive first chapter that it is this factor of expendability—an expendability that in turn derives from modern attitudes toward the stateless, the uprooted and rootless, the disadvantaged and dispossessed—that provides still another essential key to the incomprehensible dungeon of Auschwitz. The matter of surplus populations, which Rubenstein touches upon again and again, haunts this book like the shadow of a thundercloud.

But slave labor is pointless without an end product, and what did slave labor produce at Auschwitz? Of course, on one level, slaves—Jews and non-Jews—slaved to kill Jews. But this was scarcely all. One of the gaps in the knowledge of many people I have talked to is their ignorance of the fact that one of the chief functions of Auschwitz was to support a vast corporate enterprise involved in the manufacture of synthetic rubber. Anyone who has studied the Nazi period, especially that aspect of it having to do with the concentration camps, is usually both impressed and baffled by seemingly unresolvable contradictions, by the sheer ca price and irrationality of certain mandates and commands, by unexplainable cancellations of directives, by *Ordnung* in one area of operation and wild disorder in another. The SS, so celebrated for their discipline and method, seemed more often than not to have their collective heads in total disarray. Witness Himmler's order early in 1943 concerning the annihilation of the Jews; nothing would seem more unequivocal or more final. Yet this imperious command—surely one of the most awesome and terrible in history—was completely countermanded soon after it was conceived and handed down, replaced by a directive that ordered all able-bodied Jewish adult arrivals at Auschwitz not to the crematoria but to work. We can only surmise the reason for this quick reversal, but it should not take too long to conclude that pressures from I. G. Farben-Auschwitz, operators of the rubber factory, were a decisive factor in Himmler's decision, and that, at the behest of the directors of the company (which only a few years before had been helping to supply peaceful European households with tires and doormats and cushions and ashtrays), thousands of Jews each day would rejoice in their "reprieve" from the ovens at Birkenau, only to realize that they had joined the legions of the walking dead.

It is ironic that the immolation of these doomed souls (and there were among them, I think it necessary to add, hundreds of thousands of non-Jews) came to naught; we know now that for various reasons the nearby factories produced very little synthetic rubber to aid the struggles of the Wehrmacht, yet it was through no lack of effort on the part of either I. G. Farben or the SS that the enterprise was fruitless. What had been demonstrated was the way in which the bureaucratization of power in the service of a new kind of soulless bondage could cause a total domination of human beings on a level that makes the oppression of traditional, old-fashioned Western slavery—with its residue of Christian decency and compassion—seem benevolent by comparison. As Rubenstein says in an important passage:

The death-camp system became a society of total domination only when healthy inmates were kept alive and forced to become slaves rather than killed outright. . . . As long as the camps served the single function of killing prisoners, one can speak of the camps as places of mass execution but not as a new type of human society. Most of the literature on the camps has tended to stress the role of the camps as places of execution. Regrettably, few ethical theorists or religious thinkers have paid attention to the highly significant political fact that the camps were in reality a new form of human society.

And in another passage Rubenstein concludes with stunning, if grim, perception: "The camps were thus far more of a permanent threat to the human future than they would have been had they functioned solely as an exercise in mass killing. An extermination center can only manufacture corpses; a society of total domination creates a world of the living dead."

Some time ago I watched a late night discussion program on television, moderated by an entertainer named David Susskind. Assembled for the event that evening were perhaps half a dozen writers whose expertise was in the subject of the Nazis and their period, and also in the continued presence of a kind of *lumpen* underground Naziism in America. I believe most of these men were not Jewish. I remember little about the program, save for the remarkably foolish question posed by Susskind near the end. He asked in effect: "Why should you Gentiles be interested in the Nazis? Why, not being Jewish, are you concerned about the Holocaust?" There was a weak reply, *sotto voce,* from one of the participants to the effect that, well, there were others who suffered and died too, such as numerous Slavs; but the remark seemed to be ignored and I bit my tongue in embarrassment for all concerned. I was, naturally, unable to utter what I was longing to say, namely, that if the question was unbelievably fatuous the reply was shamefully feeble—*and off the mark.* Firstly, of course Mr. Susskind should be enlightened as to the vast numbers of Gentiles who shared in the same perdition visited upon the Jews, those who were starved and tortured to death at Ravensbrück and Dachau, and the droves who perished as slaves at Auschwitz. Such ignorance in a grown talk show host seemed to me by now impermissible.

But secondly, and most emphatically, the point I struggled vainly to make, murmuring to myself in the dark, was that even if this were not true—even if the Jews had been without any exception the inheritors of Hitler's hatred and destruction—the question would have been very close to indecent. I could not help think there was something paradigmatically American (or certainly non-European) in that question, with its absence of any sense of history and its vacuous unawareness of evil. By contrast how pervasive is the sense of evil in Rubenstein's essay, how urgent is the feeling that an apprehension of the devil's handiwork and an understanding of the Holocaust are the concern of Jew and non-Jew alike. We are all still immersed in this deepest pit. In *The Cunning of History,* written by a Jew and a theologian, the fact of the Holocaust as *the* cataclysmic tragedy of the Jewish people is assumed, *a priori,* as it should be, just as it is assumed that the annihilation of the Jews acquired a centrality in the Nazis' monstrous order of things. Rubenstein's analysis of the historical sources of anti-Semitism provides some of his most illuminating passages. But among the qualities that I find so compelling about Rubenstein's book, as opposed to a great deal that has been written about Auschwitz, is how, despite the foregoing, he has acquired a perspective—a philosophical and historical *spaciousness*— that has allowed him to anatomize Auschwitz with a knowledge of the titanic and sinister forces at work in history and in modern life that threaten *all* men, not only Jews. I intend no disrespect to Jewish sensibility, and at the same time am perhaps only at last replying to Mr.

Susskind, when I say how bracing it is to greet a writer who views totalitarianism as a menace to the entire human family. As an analyst of evil, Rubenstein, like Hannah Arendt, is serene and Olympian, which probably accounts for the unacceptability I have been told he has been met with in some quarters.

I have intentionally refrained until this conclusion from mentioning other important strands of Rubenstein's wide-ranging thought that are woven into the fabric of his essay: his reflections on the tangled and tormented connection between the Judeo-Christian tradition and the Holocaust, his observations on the ugly resemblance between the medical experiments at Auschwitz and those in American prisons, his fascinating consideration of the ethical and legal aspects of mass murder (his conclusion that *no* crimes were committed at Auschwitz comprises a chilling paradox), and his final meditation on civilization and the future. Also, over and over again, the problem of surplus people. Rubenstein is everywhere provocative and nowhere dull, and all of these subjects provide a vivid counterpoint to what I conceive to be his major insights. To recapitulate: perhaps because of my own involvement with slavery I have found Rubenstein's study at its most illuminating when he is dealing with Auschwitz as a phenomenon that is an inevitable continuation not only of traditional slave systems in Western society but of exploitative "wage slave" tyrannies that have kept men in bondage throughout history. The ultimate slavery of total domination that found its apotheosis in Auschwitz required only modern techniques of bureaucratization to achieve itself. Rubenstein's gift has been to show how that impulse toward domination has been embedded in our past and how, far from being extinguished, it adumbrates all of our uncertain tomorrows. Although he is wise enough to offer no specific prophecy in his pessimistic but rigorously honest essay, he leaves this reader, at least, with the feeling that the possibility of the nightmare being reborn to jeopardize the future—or perhaps even to preclude a future—is very real. Whatever that reality, and whatever befalls us, Richard Rubenstein has with a steady eye and strong mind gazed into the abyss of the immediate past. I think we risk a great deal if we do not join in his scrutiny, because not to do so would be to fail to recognize that abyss again as it becomes likely to imperil us during the onrushing years.

CHAPTER 1

Mass Death and

Contemporary Civilization

Why should anyone bother to reflect once again on the extermination of Europe's Jews by the Germans thirty years ago? The event is over and done. The world has witnessed a plethora of new horrors since that time. And, given the global threat of overpopulation, it will probably witness the death of even greater numbers by famine in the near future. Why not consign the story to the dustbin of history and be done with it?

Part of the answer lies in the fact that the popular imagination will not let the Nazi period die. People still continue to be fascinated by Hitler, Himmler, and the SS. Books about the Nazis continue to appear. They are bought in large numbers by a curious public. The Nazi period also continues to be a subject of great interest for the movies and television. Much of the popular interest is undoubtedly perverse. Some people use the Nazi story as a vehicle to express their own fantasies of sadistic domination of their peers, a domination they could never achieve in real life. Others may have an unsettling need for total submission that can more safely be expressed in fantasy than reality.

Yet, in spite of the perverse fascination, there is a sound basis for the interest in the period. The passing of time has made it increasingly evident that a hitherto unbreachable moral and political barrier in the history of Western civilization was successfully overcome by the Nazis in World War II and that henceforth the systematic, bureaucratically administered extermination of millions of citizens or subject peoples will forever be one of the capacities and temptations of government. Whether or not such a temptation is ever again exercised, the mere fact that every modern government possesses such power cannot but alter the relations between those who govern and those who are governed. This power must also alter the texture of foreign relations. According to Max Weber, "The state is a human community that (successfully) claims the monopoly of the legitimate use of force within a given territory."[1] Auschwitz has enlarged our conception of the state's capacity to do violence. A barrier has been overcome in what for millennia had been regarded as the permissible limits of political action. The Nazi period serves as a warning of what we can all too easily become were we faced with a political or an economic crisis of overwhelming proportions. The public may be fascinated by the Nazis; hopefully, it is also warned by them.

In studying the Holocaust, the extermination of Europe's Jews, it is necessary to recognize that our feelings may be strongly aroused. Both the Nazis and their victims elicit some very complicated emotional responses from most people. These feelings are important but they can add to our difficulties in arriving at an understanding of what took place. In order to understand the Holocaust, it is necessary to adopt a mental attitude that excludes all feelings of sympathy or hostility towards both the victims and the perpetrators. This is a methodological procedure and, admittedly, an extremely difficult one. Nevertheless, this bracketing is necessary, not only because of the emotions aroused by the Nazis, but also because of the ambivalent reactions Jews inevitably arouse in Western culture. In view of the fact that (a) most Europeans and Americans are the spiritual and cultural heirs of a religious tradition in which both the incarnate deity and his betrayer are Jewish and that (b) the fate of the Jews has been a primary datum used to prove the truth of Christianity from its inception, it is difficult for even the most secularized non-Jew to be without a complex mixture of feelings when confronted with Jewish disaster. These feelings are likely to include both guilt and gratification.

Nor are Jews normally capable of greater objectivity in dealing with the Holocaust. The event has challenged the very foundations of Jewish religious faith. It has reinforced all of the millennial distrust on the part of Jews for the non-Jewish world. It has also raised the exceedingly painful issue of the role of the *Judenräte*, the Jewish community councils which everywhere controlled the Jewish communities and which were used by the Germans as a principal instrument to facilitate the process of extermination.

Both Jews and non-Jews have good reasons for responding with emotion to the Holocaust. Were such a response conducive to insight concerning its political and moral consequences, there would be no reason to attempt the kind of bracketing which is here advised. However, some degree of objectivity is necessary in order to understand what took place. It is therefore necessary to withhold, insofar as it is possible, both sympathetic and hostile feelings as we attempt to arrive at some comprehension of the long-range significance of the process by which the Jews of Europe were destroyed.

It is, of course, somewhat easier to assess the meaning of the Holocaust today than it was a generation ago. During and immediately after World War II, the shock of the experience was too great. As the camps were liberated, brutal media images of survivors who seemed hardly more than walking skeletons were mixed with images of mounds of unburied corpses. The pictures hinted at the frightfulness of what had taken place, but their very horror also tended to obscure comprehension. The moral and psychological categories under which such scenes could be comprehended were hatred, cruelty, and sadism. The past was searched to find parallels with which the event could be understood. Human history is filled with incidents of rapine, robbery, and massacre. It was to such categories that the mind was initially drawn. In addition, the Jews had been the victims of degrading assault so often that there was an understandable tendency to regard the Holocaust as a contemporary manifestation of the anti-Jewish violence that had so often exploded during the two-thousand-year sojourn of the Jews in Europe.

There was also a paucity of facts. It was known that millions had been killed, but, until the German archives and the survivors' memoirs became available, it was not possible to get an accurate picture of the destruction process as a whole. Because of the total collapse of the German state in 1945, its archives became available soon after the events had taken place. Under normal conditions, many of the most important documents would never have become available. Even after having been made available, the archival material, the transcripts of the war crimes trials and the avalanche of memoirs all had to be digested. To some extent, that process is still going on. Unfortunately, whenever scholars have attempted to comprehend the Holocaust in terms of pre–twentieth-century experience, they have invariably failed to recognize the phenomenon for what it was, a thoroughly modern exercise in total domination that could only have been carried out by an advanced political community with a highly trained, tightly disciplined police and civil service bureaucracy.

As reflection replaced shock, attention shifted from a description of the mobile killing units and the death camps to the analysis of the process by which the extermination was carried out. The process was a highly complex series of acts which started simply with the bureaucratic definition of who was a Jew.[2] Once defined as a Jew, by the German state bureaucracy, a person was progressively deprived of all personal property and citizenship rights. The final step in the process came when he was eliminated altogether. The destruction process required the cooperation of every sector of German society. The bureaucrats drew up the definitions and decrees; the churches gave evidence of Aryan descent; the postal authorities carried the messages of definition, expropriation, denaturalization, and deportation; business corporations dismissed their Jewish employees and took over "Aryanized" properties; the railroads carried the victims to their place of execution, a place made available to the Gestapo and the SS by the *Wehrmacht*. To repeat, the operation required and received the participation of every major social, political, and religious institution of the German Reich.

The essential steps in the process of annihilation have been outlined by the historian and political scientist, Raul Hilberg, in his comprehensive and indispensable study, *The Destruction of the European Jews*.[3] According to Hilberg, since the fourth Christian century, there have been three fundamental anti-Jewish policies, conversion, expulsion, and annihilation. Until the twentieth century, only two of the policies were attempted in a systematic way, conversion and expulsion. Throughout the history of Christianity, there have been countless attempts to inflict violence upon Jews. These assaults were often encouraged by religious and secular authorities. Nevertheless, such outbursts, no matter how extensive, were never transformed into systematic, bureaucratically administered policies of outright extermination until World War II. According to Hilberg, the Nazis were both "innovators" and "improvisors" in their elimination of the Jews.[4]

Each of the three policies directed against Jews represented an intensification of hostile action beyond the previous step. Conversion was an attempt to subvert Jewish religious and communal institutions by securing defections to the rival faith. Expulsion was an attempt to rid a community of Jews as unwanted outsiders. Annihilation was the most radical form of expulsion. Nevertheless, there is a fundamental difference between conversion and expulsion on the one hand and extermination on the other. In conversion and expulsion, the death threat was often used as a means to an end; in extermination, killing became the end in itself.

Before the twentieth century, the Christian religious tradition was both the source of much traditional anti-Jewish hostility and an effective barrier against the final murderous step. Something changed in the twentieth century. As always, there were men who sought to rid their communities of Jews and Jewish influence, but the methods proposed were no longer limited by traditional religious or moral restraints. The rationalizations with which a massacre of the Jews could be justified were at least as old as Christendom. We need not repeat here what has been written on the subject of Christian anti-Jewish images. For our purposes, it is sufficient to note that those stereotypical images did not lead to systematic extermination until the twentieth century. There was little that the Nazis had to add to the negative image of the Jew they had inherited from Martin Luther or from the Pan-German anti-Semites of the nineteenth and early twentieth centuries. In every instance, the Jew was depicted as an enemy within the gates, a criminal and a kind of plague or species of vermin.[5] Gil Eliot has observed that such images ascribe to an adversary or a potential victim a *paranthropoid identity.*[6] As Eliot has asserted, once a human being has been stripped of his human and given a paranthropoid identity, the normal moral impediments cease to operate.

To repeat, something happened in the twentieth century that made it morally and psychologically possible to realize dreams of destructiveness that had previously been confined to fantasy. Part of the reason for the radicalization of the destructive tendencies can, of course, be found in such specific events as the defeat of Germany in World War I after four years of fighting of unprecedented violence. An element of even greater importance was the fact that the secularized culture which substituted calculating rationality for the older traditional norms in personal and group relations did not mature fully until the twentieth century. Yet another factor was the conjunction of the charismatic leadership of Adolf Hitler, the bureaucratic competence of the German police and civil service, and the mood of the German people at a particular moment in history. Himmler and Goebbels, for example, were convinced that Hitler's leadership gave the Germans a unique opportunity to eliminate the Jews that might never be repeated.[7]

All of the elements cited played their part, but more was involved. *The Holocaust was an expression of some of the most significant political, moral, religious and demographic tendencies of Western civilization in the twentieth century.* The Holocaust cannot be divorced from the very same culture of modernity that produced the two world wars and Hitler.

There were, of course, unique elements in the Holocaust. It was the first attempt by a modern, legally constituted government to pursue a policy of bureaucratically organized genocide both within and beyond its own frontiers. As such, it must be distinguished from the use of violence by a state against another state or even against its own people for the purpose of securing compliance with its policies. One of the most terrifying instances of state violence was the American nuclear attack on Hiroshima and Nagasaki at the end of World War II. Although nuclear weapons are capable of greater destructiveness than were the German death camps, there was a significant difference between Hiroshima and Auschwitz. The American assault ceased as soon as the Japanese surrendered. During World War II, German mass violence against enemy civilians was intensified *after* the victims had surrendered.[8]

Nevertheless, for all of its uniqueness, the Holocaust must be seen against the horizon of the unprecedented magnitude of violence in the twentieth century. No century in human history can match the twentieth in the sheer number of human beings slaughtered as a direct consequence of the political activity of the great states. One estimate of the humanly inflicted deaths of the twentieth century places the total at about one hundred million.[9] As fewer men have fallen prey to such natural ills as the plague and epidemic, the technology of human violence has taken up much of the slack. Those whom nature did not kill before their time were often slain by their fellowmen.

Twentieth-century mass slaughter began in earnest with World War I. About 6,000 people were killed every day for over 1,500 days.[10] The total was around ten million. World War I was the first truly modern war of the century. The civilian societies of both the Allied and the Central powers were organized in such a way that millions of ordinary people were withdrawn from their normal occupations, supplied with weapons of unprecedented destructiveness and dispatched to the battle fronts. Without the systematic organization of both population and industry, it would have been impossible to wage the kind of mass war that was fought.

A mass war has its own logic that is very different from the almost ritualistic and symbolic contests of compact units of military professionals that used to wage war on their country's behalf. Diego de Velasquez's magnificent painting, *The Surrender of Breda* (June 25, 1625), which hangs in Madrid's Prado Museum reminds us of the way European wars used to be fought: With the troops of both sides facing each other, the Dutch commander Justin of Nassau bows as he surrenders the keys of the city to the Spanish commander, the Genoese general Ambrogio Spinola. Spinola has dismounted from his horse and has placed his right hand on the shoulder of Justin as he accepts the keys. Spinola's gesture suggests knightly comradeship. There is mutual respect. The victor knows that things could have gone the other way. He is also convinced that the victory belongs to God.

In modern warfare, there is no knightly comradeship. The objective is often to deprive the enemy of his basic instrument of violence, his army. In essence, that is what General von Falkenhayn, the German commander, attempted at the Battle of Verdun. Von Falkenhayn's strategy was biological. His objective at Verdun was to exterminate as many of the enemy as possible.[11] This was a giant step towards the death camps of World War II. For the first time in memory a European nation had attempted to alter the biological rather than the military and political balance of power with an adversary. It did not occur to Von Falkenhayn that he could not slaughter the French without suffering the loss of a comparable number of his own men. The tragic story of Verdun is well known. About five hundred thousand men died on each side in a nine-month battle that ended with the battle lines more or less in the same place at the end as at the beginning. Apparently, the German military and civilian authorities did not consider so great a human sacrifice too high a price to pay for victory. It is somewhat easier to understand the resolve of the French to take their losses. They were convinced that their national existence was at stake. No similar danger threatened the Germans. They were the attackers. They were, of course, determined to win the war no matter what the cost.

From the perspective of subsequent history, Verdun offered a hint of the extent to which the leaders of Germany regarded their own people as expendable. If the German leaders were prepared to sacrifice their own people on so vast a scale, they were hardly likely to be concerned about the fate of enemy populations. Nevertheless, there is an important difference between German behavior at Verdun in 1915 and the behavior of the Nazis during World War II. There is no evidence that the Germans would have intensified their violence against their adversaries had they won World War I. Even the large-scale violence at Verdun was not a prelude to the annihilation or the permanent enslavement of the French nation. As we have noted, in World War II, the Nazis intensified their violence against their enemies after they had surrendered, especially in Eastern Europe.

Nor were the Germans alone in their indifference to the fate of large numbers of their own men. On July 1, 1916 General Sir Douglas Haig began the Battle of the Somme. By the end of the first day, the British had lost nearly sixty thousand men including half of all of the officers assigned to the battle! This was by far the worst casualty rate yet for either side. In spite of the insane casualty rate, Haig refused to desist. He was determined to break through the German lines at any cost. By the end of the year, the British offensive was a complete failure. The British lines had moved only six miles forward. Four hundred and ten thousand Britons, 500,000 Germans, and 190,000 Frenchmen were dead, and for nothing.[12]

Undoubtedly, Von Falkenhayn and Haig were convinced that they had the best of reasons for permitting the slaughter of their own troops. Both men had been entrusted by their countries with the most awesome of responsibilities, the command decisions affecting the lives of the nation's fighting men during wartime. The process by which they were selected was neither frivolous nor fortuitous. In a moment of extreme national crisis they were regarded as the best their nations could elect. Under the circumstances, their military decisions cannot be regarded as personal. They were chosen because they were trusted to make the right decisions. Those decisions were accepted. *Both the British and the German generals made the same decision: their country's young men were expendable.*

We can only ask, but so much of the history of the twentieth century points in the direction of one answer, that we must wonder whether at some level Von Falkenhayn and Haig were moved by hidden forces in themselves and their societies to preside over a mammoth bloodletting, the slaughter of their own men. We must also ask whether the ultimate objective of the attackers at Verdun and the Somme was to use wartime conditions to bring about what could not have been done under any other circumstance, the massacres themselves. It may be helpful to specify some of the underlying presuppositions that motivate the question: Von Falkenhayn and Haig were leading components of the mechanisms of destruction of their respective countries but their decisions were subject to review. Had the decisions been unacceptable, the commanders would have been speedily replaced. Furthermore, it is altogether possible that nations like individuals do not always know what they really want. Their actions may provide a better indication of what they want than the publicly stated declarations of their leaders. Both Haig and Von Falkenhayn were convinced that the blood sacrifices were indispensable to victory; so too were those who ratified their decisions. For three centuries the peoples of Europe had exported their surplus populations* to North and South America, thereby putting off the day when the inexorable fatalities to which Thomas Malthus pointed finally overtook them. In the nineteenth century, Europe also began to export its sons to participate in the newer imperialist ventures in Africa and Asia. In the twentieth century, the American frontier was closing and, in spite of the continuing emigration, population continued to grow in most European countries. Is it not possible that some automatic, self-regulating mechanism in European society was blindly yet purposefully experimenting by means of the war with alternative means of population reduction? It has been observed that population control mechanisms often come into play when the number of animals in some species begins to get out of hand.[13] Could it have been that both the Allies and the

* It is important to note that the concept of a surplus population is not absolute. An underpopulated nation can have a redundant population if it is so organized that a segment of its able-bodied human resources cannot be utilized in any meaningful economic or social role.

Central Powers were in the grip of historical forces that were acting behind them without their conscious knowledge?

Obviously a definitive answer to the questions raised would require greater historical, psychological, and demographic scholarship than is now available. Yet, we do know of a partial parallel. There is evidence that Hitler welcomed World War II because of the opportunity it provided him to institute extermination programs against groups he regarded as undesirable. The law granting a "mercy death" to the mentally incompetent and the "incurably sick" was promulgated on September 1, 1939.[14] The first extermination program of the German government was initiated the very day the war broke out. It was directed not against Jews but against mentally incompetent Germans. Also, in his Reichstag speech of January 31, 1939 Hitler promised Europe's Jews that if war broke out they would not survive.[15] Given Hitler's style, that was his way of saying that war would break out and that the Jews would perish. Goebbels wrote in his diary that "the war made possible for us the solution of a whole series of problems that could never have been solved in normal times."[16] Is it possible that one difference between the Nazi elite and the World War I elites that chose Haig and Von Falkenhayn for their respective posts was that the leading Nazis knew why they had really chosen the path of war?

The mass death that took place in the West during World War I was prelude to the carnage that took place in the Russian sphere as a result of revolution, civil war, demographic violence, and large-scale famine. Exact figures are unavailable but an estimated two to three million died as a result of hard violence and six to eight million as a result of long-term privation. According to Gil Eliot, the foundations of twentieth-century military slaughter on a mass scale were laid during World War I; the foundations of mass civilian slaughter were laid immediately thereafter, especially in Central and Eastern Europe, the very area in which the Jews were to perish during the Second World War.[17] Nor ought we to neglect to mention the Turkish massacre of about one million Armenians during World War I, perhaps the first full-fledged attempt by a modern state to practice disciplined, methodically organized genocide.[18] The list of victims of twentieth-century mass slaughter also includes those who perished in the Sino-Japanese War and the Spanish Civil War; the millions who were killed in the various Stalinist purges, as well as those who died in the man-made famines which resulted from Stalin's slaughter of peasants who resisted collectivization between 1929 and 1933; the Russian and Polish prisoners of war exterminated by the Germans; the Russian prisoners of war who escaped death at the hands of the Germans only to be murdered when they returned home; those who perished at Hiroshima and Nagasaki, and the victims of the wars and revolutions of Southeast Asia.[19] The list is by no means complete. It is, however, sufficient to place the Holocaust within the context of the phenomenon of twentieth-century mass death. Never before have human beings been so expendable. Perhaps the spirit of the twentieth century has seldom been expressed as well as by Maxim Gorky's tale of the peasant who confessed that he had killed another peasant and stolen his cow during the Russian Revolution. The murderer was greatly worried that he might be prosecuted for theft. When asked whether he was afraid that he might also be prosecuted for murder, the peasant replied: "That is nothing; people now come cheaply."[20]

When the peace treaties that brought World War I to an end were finally signed, Europe was confronted with a new problem of enormous consequences for the mass murders of World War II, the problem of the *apatrides* or stateless persons. With the dissolution of the Hapsburg and Romanov empires, Central and Eastern Europe was divided into a group of successor states such as Poland, Yugoslavia, Hungary, and Czechoslovakia. Each of the successor states contained large numbers of people who belonged to the national minorities, such as the Croats in Yugoslavia, the Ukrainians in Poland and the Sudeten Germans in Czechoslovakia. At the peace conferences an attempt was made to guarantee the political and legal rights of these minorities. With the exception of Czechoslovakia, all of the successor states signed under protest the treaties protecting the rights of their minorities. They regarded the treaties as unwarranted interference in their internal affairs. As Hannah Arendt has pointed out, in spite of the treaty guarantees, none of the national minorities could either trust or be trusted by the states of which they were technically citizens.[21] To make matters worse, the unfortunate fact that the minority guarantees were deemed necessary was itself recognition that only persons belonging to the dominant state nationality, such as the Poles in Poland or the Hungarians in Hungary, could count upon the full protection of the political and legal institutions of the states in which they were citizens. Miss Arendt has observed that, with the signing of the minorities' treaties after World War I, the transformation of the state from an institution of law into an instrument of the dominant national community had been completed.[22] When Hitler proclaimed that "right is what is good for the German *Volk*," he was only expressing crudely a fact that had become a part of the political condition of millions of Europeans. The current violence between Catholics and Protestants in Northern Ireland and Greek and Turk in Cyprus is entirely understandable in the light of the experience of Europe's national minorities after World War I. The Catholics of Northern Ireland can neither trust nor identify with a Protestant-dominated government; the Protestants fear any move that might eventually dissolve their political community in the predominantly Catholic Irish Republic. In spite of any possible good intentions of the Catholic majority in the Irish Republic or the Protestant majority in the north, both groups have good reason for apprehension about being a permanent minority. A similar dilemma confronts both Greeks and Turks on Cyprus as well as the Israelis and the Palestinian Arabs.

After World War I, the minorities in the successor states felt that they had been deprived of something they regarded as indispensable to human dignity, full membership in a stable political community. Yet, though disadvantaged, most of these minorities were in reality only half stateless. They did possess at least nominal membership in a political body. When, for example, they traveled abroad, they were protected by a Polish, Czech, Yugoslav, or Romanian passport. In some respects, a Ukrainian with a Polish passport was better off in Paris than Warsaw. The French police did not discriminate against bearers of valid passports in the same way that the Polish police might at home. Such a person had the formal protection of the Polish government. There were limits to the way the French police might deal with him. Actually, some passports were issued between the wars with the understanding that their bearers could use them anywhere but in the country that issued them.

The situation of the Ukrainian with a Polish passport would have changed drastically had the Polish government suddenly canceled his citizenship. He would have become a man without a country and, as such, without *any* meaningful human rights whatsoever. In the twenties and thirties *denaturalization* and *denationalization* were increasingly used by governments as ways of getting rid of citizens they deemed undesirable. One of the first large groups to suffer denationalization were the White Russian opponents of the Bolshevik regime who escaped to the West. Approximately one million five hundred thousand Russians were deprived of their citizenship by the Soviet government in the aftermath of the revolution and the civil war period. In the civil wars of the twentieth century, there has been little if any reconciliation between opposing sides. Expulsion and extermination have often been the preferred methods of the victors in dealing with the losing side. The denationalized White Russians were followed by the Spanish republicans, the Armenians and, of course, the Jews.[23]

As the stateless refugees entered the countries of the West, especially France, it was soon discovered that these were people who could neither be repatriated nor granted citizenship by the host country. The stateless were truly men without any political community. No country wanted them or cared about their fate. As Miss Arendt has shown, an *apatride* could more easily better his status in the host country by committing a minor crime than by remaining fully law abiding. The law gave him no rights until he violated it. He was then treated as an ordinary petty criminal and given the same legal rights to a fair trial as any native. Even in prison, he was entitled to the same rights as any other prisoner. The *apatride* reverted to the status of a person with no rights only when he completed his sentence.

In dealing with the *apatride* who could not be repatriated, the host country could either suffer his presence at liberty, subject at all times to police surveillance, or it could set up concentration camps in which to detain him. In either case, the *apatride*, although not a criminal, was for all practical purposes an outlaw. He was subject to the kind of police surveillance and control that was not in turn subject to judicial review. Stateless persons were thus among the first Europeans in the twentieth century to experience unrestricted police domination. Once the police tasted the freedom of dominating one class of men unhindered by judicial process or legal restraint, they sought to extend their power to others. This process reached its zenith in Nazi Germany towards the end of the war when the power of the Gestapo and the SS over the German people was almost completely unhindered by any competing institution.

While individual *apatrides* were permitted to pursue whatever manner of life they could find as refugees within the urban centers of the host countries, as soon as large numbers of *apatrides*, such as the veterans of the Spanish Republican army, entered a host country *en masse*, they were placed in detention camps which were in reality concentration camps.[24]

The concentration camps for the *apatrides* served much the same purpose as did the original Nazi camps in 1933 and 1934. In the popular mind, the first Nazi camps conjure up images of wild sadism by brutal, brown-shirted storm troopers The images are, of course, well deserved, but they tend to hinder precise understanding of the development of the camps as a legal and political institution.

Initially, the concentration camps were established to accommodate detainees who had been placed under "protective custody" *(Schützhaft)* by the Nazi regime.[25] Those arrested were people whom the regime wished to detain although there was no clear legal justification for so doing. Almost all of the original detainees were German communists, not Jews. Had the Nazis' political prisoners been brought before a German court in the first year or two of Hitler's regime, the judiciary would have been compelled to dismiss the case. This was not because the German judiciary was anti-Nazi, but because it was bureaucratic in structure. In the early stages of the Nazi regime, there was no formula in law to cover all the political prisoners the Nazis wanted to arrest. This problem was solved by holding them under "protective custody" and setting up camps outside of the regular prison system to receive them. Incidentally, the American government did something very similar when it interned Japanese-American citizens during World War II. They had committed no crime. No court would have convicted them. Prison was not the place to detain them. Happily, as bad as were the American concentration camps, they were infinitely better than the German counterparts.

Like the original political prisoners in the German camps, there was no legal basis for the detention of the *apatrides*. Yet, the host countries' leaders were convinced that it was in their nation's interest to hold them. Camps were established for those who had no status in law and for whom no law existed that could justify their being held. The unifying bond between the *apatrides* and the first prisoners in the German concentration camps was that both groups were outlaws.

Neither the *apatrides* nor the German political prisoners were outlaws because of any crime they had committed, but because their status had been altered by their country's civil service or police bureaucracy. They had been deprived of all political status by bureaucratic definition. As such, they had become *superfluous men*. Those *apatrides* in the detention camps were among the living dead. Sooner or later, most of the living dead were destined to join that vast company Gil Eliot has called "the nation of the dead," the millions who perished by large-scale human violence in this bloodiest of centuries.[26] What made the *apatrides* superfluous was no lack of ability, intelligence, or potential social usefulness. There were gifted physicians, lawyers, scholars, and technicians among them. Nevertheless, in most instances no established political community had any use for the legitimate employment of their gifts. This was especially true of the Jewish refugees, but they were by no means alone.

Before World War II, the number of stateless persons increased with every passing year. Statesmen and police officials were agreed that a solution to the problem had to be found. The stateless could neither be assimilated nor, in most cases, expelled. International conferences on the "refugee problem" were held, but to no avail.[27] There seemed to be no solution. In reality, there was a "solution" that was obvious to Hitler. When one has surplus livestock that are a drain on resources, one gets rid of them. Neither Hitler nor Stalin saw any reason why people ought to be treated differently. The "solution" had logic on its side, yet there remained a sentimental obstacle: In the prewar period, it was not yet possible to exterminate surplus people the way a farmer might kill off surplus cattle.

We who live in the post–World War II era have seen the birth of an altogether different moral universe. Perhaps the new universe was expressed most succinctly not by a German but by a Briton, Lord Moyne, the British High Commissioner in Egypt in 1944. When informed by Joel Brand, a Hungarian Jewish emissary, that there was a possibility of saving one million Hungarian Jews from extermination at Auschwitz through Adolf Eichmann's infamous "blood for trucks" deal, Lord Moyne replied, "What shall I do with those million Jews? Where shall I put them?"[28] Lord Moyne and his government understood that Hitler's "final solution" was the most convenient way of solving the problem of disposing of one group of surplus people for themselves as well as for the Germans. The British government was by no means averse to the "final solution" as long as the Germans did most of the dirty work.

Even the Nazis, save perhaps for Hitler and some ultraextremists, did not initially contemplate extermination as the preferred method of "solving" the Jewish problem. They first tested expulsion and forced emigration as alternatives. It is likely that Hitler never contemplated any "solution" other than killing. Nevertheless, until the start of the war, the Nazis gave the Jews every encouragement to leave Germany, albeit stripped of almost all of their possessions. When the Germans took over Austria, they continued this policy. They set up a *Zentralstelle für Jüdische Auswanderung* whose function was to process Austrian Jews for mass expulsion on an assembly-line basis. Even after the war began, there was talk in SS circles about a postwar settlement of millions of Jews in Madagascar. In the light of subsequent events, it is likely that the Madagascar scheme was never a serious option but served to camouflage the more radical intentions of the Nazi elite.[29]

The Nazi elite clearly understood that the Jews were truly a *surplus people* whom nobody wanted and whom they could dispose of as they pleased. Hilberg quotes a memorandum written by Joachim von Ribbentrop, the German Foreign Minister, and addressed to Hitler concerning a conversation he had on December 9, 1938, with Georges Bonnet, the French foreign minister, on the question of Jewish emigration from Germany:

The Jewish Question: After I had told M. Bonnet that I could not discuss the question officially with him, he said that he only wanted to tell me privately how great an interest was being taken in France in a solution of the Jewish problem. To my question as to what France's interest might be, M. Bonnet said that in the first place they did not want to receive any more Jews from Germany and whether we could not take some sort of measures to keep them from coming to France and that in the second place France had to ship 10,000 Jews somewhere else; they were actually thinking of Madagascar for this.
I replied to M. Bonnet that we all wanted to get rid of our Jews but that the difficulties lay in the fact that no country wished to receive them.[30]

It is likely that Von Ribbentrop knew that there was a simple way to keep Jews "from coming to France" and that eventually M. Bonnet would be obliged.

The Nazis insisted that the protests emanating from the so-called democracies concerning German treatment of the Jews were not without a strong element of hypocrisy. This theme recurs frequently in Nazi sources. For example, on December 13, 1942, Goebbels wrote in his diary, "At bottom, I believe that both the English and the Americans are happy that we are exterminating the Jewish riffraff."[31] The more one studies the literature of the period, the more difficult it is to avoid the conclusion that Goebbels was right, at least in his estimation of the British, but also to some degree the American government.

When we look for the problem the British were attempting to "solve" by their not entirely passive cooperation with the Germans in the extermination of the Jews, it is clear that they were seeking to protect their disintegrating imperial domain east of Suez, especially in India. Beneath all pretensions to imperial glory, the British had their own economic and political reasons for being in India. The Indians understandably wanted to be rid of them, and the problem of maintaining Britain's position in India was for a long time a preoccupation of English statesmen. At one point, some British bureaucrats in India contemplated "administrative massacres" as a means of terrorizing the Indians and maintaining their own tenuous hold.[32] While the British government was unwilling to follow through on the suggested "administrative massacres" in India, they were entirely willing to permit the Germans to practice such massacres on their behalf. Every Jew whom the Germans murdered was one less Jew who might enter Palestine, thereby adding to the political instability of the region immediately adjacent to the Suez Canal, England's life line to India. Nor was Britain's role merely that of a passive spectator deriving benefit from the dirty work done by others. Many of her actions bordered on active complicity. This was especially true of those instances in which British warships forced ships carrying Jewish refugees to return to Europe and what was known to be certain extermination rather than permit the refugees even the temporary haven of detention camps in Palestine. The British government was spared the moral dilemma of whether or not to murder the fleeing Jews to "solve" its imperial problem in the Middle East, but the weight of available evidence points to the extent to which it was willing to cooperate with the Germans. As the Nazis rounded up Europe's Jews for the "final solution," the British government, with full and accurate knowledge of what was taking place in the extermination centers, ordered its Navy forcibly to prevent any Jews from escaping from Europe to Palestine.

It would be interesting to examine the archives of the British Foreign Office as they relate to this question. Because the British were technically victorious, many of the most revealing documents may never become available. Yet, Hilberg has found a document that raises some interesting questions. During the period in 1944 in which the Nazis were sending over seven hundred and fifty thousand Hungarian Jews to

Auschwitz, Chaim Weizmann, who was to become Israel's first President, transmitted two messages to Anthony Eden, the British foreign secretary, requesting that the gassing installations and railroad lines at Birkenau, Auschwitz's extermination facility, be subjected to aerial bombardment. Two months passed before Weizmann received a reply. In the meantime several hundred thousand Jews were killed at Auschwitz-Birkenau. The reply dated September 1, 1944, reads:

My dear Dr. Weizmann:

You will remember that on the 6th of July you discussed with the Foreign Secretary the Camp of Birkenau in Upper Silesia, and the atrocities that were being committed there by Germans against Hungarian and other Jews. You enquired whether any steps could be taken to put a stop to, or even to mitigate those massacres, and you suggested that something might be achieved by bombing the camps and, also, if it was possible, the railway lines leading to them.

As he promised, Mr. Eden immediately put the proposal to the Secretary of State for Air. The matter received the most careful consideration of the Air Staff, but I am sorry to have to tell you that, in view of the very great technical difficulties involved, we have no option but to refrain from pursuing the proposal in present circumstances.

I realize that this decision will prove a disappointment for you, but you may feel fully assured that the matter was most thoroughly investigated.

Yours sincerely,
Richard Law[33]

At the time of the British refusal, the Allies had air supremacy over Europe. Hungary was being bombed almost daily. The British were quite willing to fire bomb Dresden, annihilating over one hundred thousand civilians to no military purpose, but they were unwilling even to attempt to drop a few bombs to stop the murderous traffic to Auschwitz. Unfortunately, the archival material is unavailable with which we might catch a glimpse of the policy discussions that were behind the letter to Weizmann. Nor ought we to forget the willingness of the British government to squander the lives of their own young men in World War I. If they held the lives of their own youth so cheaply, is it at all surprising that they held the lives of those who might conceivably have created political difficulties for them as of no account whatsoever?

My point in emphasizing British complicity in the extermination project is not to indulge in any sort of moral denunciation of the British. The incident is significant a generation later because, like Germany, Great Britain is one of the great centers of the civilization of the Western world. One of the least helpful ways of understanding the Holocaust is to regard the destruction process as the work of a small group of irresponsible criminals who were atypical of normal statesmen and who somehow gained control of the German people, forcing them by terror and the deliberate stimulation of religious and ethnic hatred to pursue a barbaric and retrograde policy that was thoroughly at odds with the great traditions of Western civilization.

On the contrary, *we are more likely to understand the Holocaust if we regard it as the expression of some of the most profound tendencies of Western civilization in the twentieth century.* Given Britain's imperial commitments, Europe's Jews were as much a superfluous population for Great Britain as they were for Germany. In the moral universe of the twentieth century, the most "rational" and least costly "solution" of the problem of disposing of a surplus population is unfortunately extermination. Properly executed, extermination is the problem-solving strategy least likely to entail unanticipated feedback hazards for its planners. From a purely bureaucratic perspective, the extermination of the Jews of Europe was the "final solution" for the British as well as the Germans.

CHAPTER 2

Bureaucratic Domination

Usually the progress in death-dealing capacity achieved in the twentieth century has been described in terms of technological advances in weaponry. Too little attention has been given to the advances in social organization that allowed for the effective use of the new weapons. In order to understand how the moral barrier was crossed that made massacre in the millions possible, it is necessary to consider the importance of bureaucracy in modern political and social organization. The German sociologist Max Weber was especially cognizant of its significance. Writing in 1916, long before the Nazi party came to prominence in German politics, Weber observed:

When fully developed, bureaucracy stands . . . under the principle of *sine ira ac studio* (without scorn and bias). *Its specific nature which is welcomed by capitalism develops the more perfectly the more bureaucracy is 'dehumanized,'* the more completely it succeeds in eliminating from official business love, hatred, and all purely personal, irrational and emotional elements which escape calculation. *This is the specific nature of bureaucracy and it is appraised as its special virtue.*"[1] (Italics added.)

Weber also observed:

The decisive reason for the advance of bureaucratic organization has always been its purely technical superiority over any other kind of organization. *The fully developed bureaucratic mechanism compares with other organizations exactly as does the machine with the nonmechanical modes of organization.*

Precision, speed, unambiguity, knowledge of the files, continuity, discretion, unity, strict subordination, reduction of friction and of material and personal costs—these are raised to the optimum point in the strictly bureaucratic organization."[2] (Italics added.)

Weber stressed "the fully developed bureaucratic mechanism." He was aware of the fact that actual bureaucracies seldom achieve the level of efficiency of the "ideal type" he had constructed.[3] Nevertheless, he saw clearly that bureaucracy was a machine capable of effective action and was as indifferent to "all purely personal . . . elements which escape calculation" as any other machine.

In his time Karl Marx looked forward to the eventual domination of the proletariat over the body politic because of its indispensability to the working process. Max Weber was convinced that political domination would rest with whoever controlled the bureaucratic apparatus because of its indisputable superiority as an instrument for the organization of human action. But, to the best of my knowledge, even Weber never entertained the possibility that the police and civil service bureaucracies could be used as a death machine to eliminate millions who had been rendered superfluous by definition. Even Weber seems to have stopped short of foreseeing state-sponsored massacres as one of the "dehumanized" capacities of bureaucracy.

Almost from the moment they came to power, the Nazis understood the bureaucratic mechanism they controlled. When they first came to power, there were a large number of widely publicized bullying attacks on Jews throughout Germany, especially by the SA, the brown-shirted storm troopers. However, it was soon recognized that improperly organized attacks by individuals or small groups actually hindered the process leading to administrative massacre. The turning from sporadic bullying to systematic anonymous terror paralleled the decline in influence of the SA and the rise of Heinrich Himmler and the SS. Himmler does not seem to have been a sadist. During the war, he did not like to watch killing operations and became upset when he did.[4] But, *Himmler was the perfect bureaucrat.* He did what he believed was his duty *sine ira et studio*, without bias or scorn. He recognized that the task assigned to his men, mass extermination, was humanly speaking exceedingly distasteful. On several occasions, he praised the SS for exercising an obedience so total that they overcame the feelings men would normally have when engaged in mass murder. The honor of the SS, he held, involved the ability to overcome feelings of compassion and achieve what was in fact perfect bureaucratic objectivity.[5]

Himmler objected to private acts of sadism, but his reasons were organizational rather than moral. He understood that individual and small group outbursts diminished the efficiency of the SS. One of his most important "contributions" to the Nazi regime was to encourage the systematization of SS dominance and terror in the concentration camps. At the beginning of Hitler's rule, Himmler, as head of the SS, was subordinate to Ernst Röhm, the head of the SA, the storm troopers. Himmler's position was transformed when Hitler ordered Röhm murdered on June 30, 1934. He ceased to be a subordinate. In the aftermath of the Röhm *Putsch*, there was a general downgrading of the SA. SA guards were removed from the concentration camps. Their places were taken by Himmler's SS.[6] By 1936 Himmler was appointed *Reichsführer SS* and *Chef der Deutschen Polizei*. He then dominated the entire German police apparatus.

One of the examples of Himmler's organizing ability was his involvement in the concentration camp at Dachau which he founded in 1933. Originally, there was little to distinguish Dachau from any of the early "wild" Nazi camps. Under Himmler's guidance, Dachau became a model for the systematically managed camps of World War II. Under his direction, the sporadic terror of the "wild" camps was replaced by impersonal, systematized terror. Much of the systematization was carried out with Himmler's approval by Theodor Eicke who became commandant at Dachau in June 1933.[7] Eicke had spent most of his career in police administration. His organization of the camp was modern and professional. His "discretionary camp regulations," issued on October 1, 1933, provided for a strictly graded series of punishments including solitary confinement and both corporal and capital punishment for offending prisoners. When corporal punishment was inflicted, Eicke's directives provided that the punishment be carried out by several SS guards in the presence of the other guards, the prisoners and the commandant. In a report dated May 8, 1935, Eicke's successor as Dachau commandant wrote to Himmler that individual guards were "forbidden to lay hands on a prisoner or to have private conversations with them."[8] The intent of Eicke's regulations was to eliminate all arbitrary punishment by individual guards and to replace it with impersonal, anonymous punishment. The impersonal nature of the transaction was heightened by the fact that any guard could be called on to inflict punishment. Even if a guard was struck by a prisoner, he could not retaliate personally, at least insofar as the regulations were concerned. Like everything else at the camps, under Himmler punishment was bureaucratized and depersonalized. Bureaucratic mass murder reached its fullest development when gas chambers with a capacity for killing two thousand people at a time were installed at Auschwitz. As Hannah Arendt has observed, the very size of the chambers emphasized the complete depersonalization of the killing process.[9]

Under Himmler, there was no objection to cruelty, provided it was disciplined and systematized. This preference was also shared by the German civil service bureaucracy. According to Hilberg, the measure that gave the civil service bureaucrats least difficulty in exterminating their victims was the imposition of a starvation diet.[10] In a bureaucratically controlled society where every individual's ration can be strictly determined, starvation is the ideal instrument of "clean" violence. A few numbers are manipulated on paper in an office hundreds of miles away from the killing centers and millions can be condemned to a prolonged and painful death. In addition, both the death rate and the desired level of vitality of the inmates can easily be regulated by the same bureaucrats.

As starvation proceeds, the victim's appearance is so drastically altered that by the time death finally releases him, he hardly seems like a human being worth saving. The very manner of death confirms the rationalization with which the killing was justified in the first place. The Nazis assigned the paranthropoid identity of a *Tiermensch*, a subhuman, to their victims. By the time of death that identity seemed like a self-fulfilling prophecy. Yet, the bureaucrat need lose no sleep over his victims. He never confronts the results of his distinctive kind of homicidal violence.

A crucial turning point in the transformation of outbursts of hatred into systematized violence occurred in the aftermath of the infamous *Kristallnacht*, the Nazi anti-Jewish riots of November 10, 1938. It is generally agreed that the riots were an unsuccessful attempt on the part of Propaganda Minister Joseph Goebbels and the SA to gain a role in the anti-Jewish process. On November 9, 1938, a young Jew, Herschel Grynzpan assassinated Legationsrat Ernst vom Rath in the German embassy in Paris. At Goebbels's instigation, SA formations set out to burn down every synagogue in Germany.[11] Jewish stores were burned and looted and Jews were attacked throughout the country.

The SS was not informed that the operation was to take place. When Himmler heard that Goebbels had instigated a pogrom, he ordered the detention of twenty thousand Jews in concentration camps under his control and ordered the police and the SS to prevent widespread looting. According to Hilberg, Himmler dictated a file memorandum in which he expressed his distaste for the Goebbels pogrom.[12]

In the wake of the *Kristallnacht*, there was widespread negative reaction against the pogrom from such leading Nazis as Goering, Economy Minister Walter Funk and the German Ambassador to the United States, Hans Dieckhoff.[13] Goering was especially vehement in his opposition to *Einzelaktionen*, undisciplined individual actions. He expressed his opposition to pogroms and riots which led to unfavorable foreign repercussions and which permitted the mob to run loose. Goering's feelings were shared by the entire German state bureaucracy. This was simply not the way to "solve" the Jewish problem. According to Hilberg, the effect of the Nazi outrages of the thirties on the state bureaucracy was to convince the Nazi and the non-Nazi bureaucrats alike that measures against the Jews had to be taken in a rational organized way.[14] Every step in the *methodical* elimination of the Jews had to be planned and carried out in a thoroughly *disciplined* manner. Henceforth, there would be neither emotional outbursts nor improvisations. The same meticulous care that goes into the manufacture of a Leica or a Mercedes was to be applied to the problem of eliminating the Jews. *Kristallnacht* was the last occasion when Jews had to fear street violence in Germany. Henceforth no brown-shirted bullies would assail them. Hilberg points out that when a decree was issued in September 1941 requiring Jews to wear the yellow star, Martin Bormann, the Chief of the Party Chancellery, issued strict orders against the molestation of the Jews as beneath the dignity of the Nazi movement.[15] "Law and order" prevailed. There were no further state-sponsored incidents. The hoodlums were banished and the bureaucrats took over. Only then was it possible to contemplate the extermination of millions. A machinery was set up that was devoid of both love and hatred. *It was only possible to overcome the moral barrier that had in the past prevented the systematic riddance of surplus populations when the project was taken out of the hands of bullies and hoodlums and delegated to bureaucrats.*

When Max Weber wrote about bureaucratic domination, he did not have the Nazis in mind, nor was he proposing a prescription for slaughter. Yet, almost everything Weber wrote on the subject of bureaucracy can in retrospect be read as a description of the way the bureaucratic heirarchies of the Third Reich "solved" their Jewish problem. Furthermore, Weber's writings on bureaucracy are part of a larger attempt to understand the social and political structure and the values of modern Western civilization. Although there were bureaucracies in ancient China, Egypt, and Imperial Rome, the full development of bureaucracy in the Christian West came about as the result of the growth of a certain ethos that was in turn the outcome of fundamental tendencies in occidental religion. Bureaucracy can be understood as a structural and organizational expression of the related processes of *secularization, disen-*

chantment of the world, and *rationalization.* The secularization process involves the liberation of ever wider areas of human activity from religious domination.[16] Disenchantment of the world occurs when "there are no mysterious forces that come into play, but rather that one can, in principle, master all things by calculation."[17] Rationalization involves "the methodical attainment of a definitely given and practical end by means of an increasingly precise calculation of adequate means."[18]

The earliest culture in which the world was "disenchanted" was the biblical world of the Israelites. When the author of Genesis wrote "In the beginning God created heaven and earth" (Gen. 1:1), he was expressing that disenchantment. Creation was seen as devoid of independent divine or magical forces which men had to appease. The world was seen as created by a supra-mundane Creator. As long as men came to terms with the Creator, the world was theirs to do with as they pleased. No interference need be feared from powers immanent in the natural order. On the contrary, Adam is enjoined to "subdue" the earth and to "have dominion" over it. (Gen.1:28) As Peter Berger has pointed out, the biblical attitude that nature is devoid of magic or mysterious forces was extended to the political order.[19] Thus, when David the king takes Bath Sheba in adultery and arranges to have her husband, Uriah the Hittite, slain in battle, he is denounced by Nathan the prophet. In the ancient Near East, the king was thought to be either a deity in his own right or to incarnate divinity by virtue of his office. By denouncing David, Nathan was insisting that the king was only a man, albeit one of preeminent importance, and that he was as subject to God's law as any other man. In ancient Israel, both the natural and the political orders were "disenchanted." The domain of divinity was relegated to the heavenly sphere. A beginning was made towards the secularization of the human order. The biblical world initiates the secularization process which finally culminates in the most extreme forms of secular disenchantment in modern political organization.[20] There is, of course, a profound difference between the biblical conception of the political order and the modern conception. In the biblical world, all of human activity stands under the judgment of a righteous and omnipotent deity;

in the modern world, the righteous and omnipotent deity has disappeared *for all practical purposes.* Man is alone in the world, free to pursue whatever ends he chooses "by means of an increasingly precise calculation of adequate means."

Berger maintains that the Christian doctrine of the incarnation, that Christ is simultaneously perfectly human and perfectly divine, was an attempt to find once again an intrinsic link between the supramundane realm of divinity and the desacralized human order which had become devoid of magic or mysterious forces.[21] A partial attempt to *reenchant* the world took place in Roman Catholicism. Although the world is not the dwelling place of deities and spirits in Catholicism, it is at least a realm in which God's presence might indwell in his saints as well as in sacred space and sacred time.

Protestantism violently rejected the Catholic attempt at reenchantment.[22] Its insistence on the radical transcendence of the one sovereign Creator and his utter withdrawal from the created order was far more thoroughgoing than the earlier Jewish attempt at disenchantment. Martin Luther proclaimed that the world was so hopelessly corrupted by sin and so totally devoid of the saving presence of God, that the Devil is in fact Lord of this world. The Protestant insistence that man is saved by faith alone *(sola fidei),* rather than works, separates man's activities in the empirical world from the realm of divinity with a remorseless logic to which biblical Judaism had pointed but did not reach.

It was the land of the Reformation that became the land in which bureaucracy was first perfected in its most completely objective form. The land of the Reformation was also the land where bureaucracy was able to create its most thoroughly secularized, rationalized, and dehumanized "achievement," the death camp. Before men could acquire the "dehumanized" attitude of bureaucracy in which "love, hatred, and all purely personal, irrational, and emotional elements" are eliminated in one's dealings with one's fellowmen, the disenchantment process had to become culturally predominant; God and the world had to be so radically disjoined that it became possible to treat both the political and the natural order with an uncompromisingly dispassionate objectivity.

When one contrasts the attitude of the savage who cannot leave the battlefield until he performs some kind of appeasement ritual to his slain enemy with the assembly-line manufacture of corpses by the millions at Auschwitz, we get an idea of the enormous religious and cultural distance Western man has traversed in order to create so unique a social and political institution as the death camp.

When I suggest that the cultural ethos that permitted the perfection of bureaucratic mass murder was most likely to develop in the land of Luther, my intention is not to blame Protestantism for the death camps. Nor is it my intention to plead for a utopian end to bureaucracy. It must not be forgotten that the Protestant insistence upon the radical transcendence of a supramundane God, which was the indispensable theological precondition of both the secularization process and disenchantment of the world, was biblical in origin. Furthermore, Jewish emancipation in Europe following the French revolution was a direct result of the more or less successful overthrow of a feudal society of inherited, often mystified status by a secular society in which men were bound to each other primarily by contractual relations. The very same secularization process which led to Jewish emancipation led to the death camps one hundred and fifty years later. It is, however, crucial that we recognize that the process of secularization that led to the bureaucratic objectivity required for the death camps was an essential and perhaps inevitable outcome of the *religious* traditions of the Judeo-Christian west. One of the most paradoxical aspects of biblical religion is that the liberation of significant areas of human activity from religious domination, which we call secularization, was the cultural outcome of biblical religion itself rather than a negation of it.[23]

This point is especially important in correcting the point of view that mistakenly regards the Nazi extermination of the Jews as an antireligious explosion of pagan values in the heart of the Judeo-Christian world.[24] When Nazism is seen in such a light, its interpreters are quick to counsel a turning away from "modern paganism" and a return to the values of Judeo-Christian culture as the only way to avoid a barbaric repetition of the "pagan" explosion some time in the future. There may be good reasons for a "return" to Judeo-Christian values, but the prevention of future extermination projects is not likely to be one of them. Weber's studies on bureaucracy and his related studies on Protestantism, capitalism, and disenchantment of the world are important in demonstrating how utterly mistaken is any view that would isolate Nazism and its supreme expression, bureaucratic mass murder and the bureaucratically administered society of total domination, from the mainstream of Western culture.

One mistake often made by those who appeal to the humanistic ideals of the Judeo-Christian tradition is the failure to distinguish between the *manifest values* a tradition asserts to be binding and the *ethos* generated by that same tradition. The Judeo-Christian tradition is said to proclaim an ethic in which every man is possessed of an irreducible element of human dignity as a child of God. Nevertheless, beyond all conscious intent, it has produced a secularization of consciousness involving an abstract, dehumanized, calculating rationality that can eradicate every vestige of that same human dignity in all areas of human interchange. Furthermore, of the two elements that together form the basis of Western culture, the classical humanism of Greco-Roman paganism and the Judeo-Christian religious tradition, it is the biblical tradition that has led to the secularization of consciousness, disenchantment of the world, methodical conduct (as in both Protestantism and capitalism), and, finally, bureaucratic objectivity. Nor ought we to be surprised that the bureaucratic objectivity of the Germans was paralleled by the diplomatic objectivity of the British. They were both nourished by the same culture. *The culture that made the death camps possible was not only indigenous to the West but was an outcome, albeit unforeseen and unintended, of its fundamental religious traditions.*

In order to understand more fully the connection between bureaucracy and mass death, it will be necessary to return to the *apatrides*. They were the first modern Europeans who had become politically and legally superfluous and for whom the most "rational" way of dealing with them was ultimately murder. A majority of the *apatrides* had lost their political status by a process of bureaucratic definition, denationalization. Miss

Arendt lists a World War I measure of the French (1915) as the first such measure. It was relatively innocent. It provided that naturalized citizens of enemy origin who had neglected to disavow their original citizenship were to be deprived of their French citizenship. A year later Portugal deprived all Portugese citizens born of a German father of citizenship. In 1922 Belgium canceled the citizenship of persons who had committed "antinational acts" during World War I. Under Mussolini, Italy followed suit by passing a law providing for the denationalization of all those who were "unworthy of Italian citizenship" or who were a menace to public order. Characteristically, the Italians were reluctant to put the law into effect even against enemies of the Fascist regime once it was on the books. The Italians do not seem to have been able to achieve the objectivity of their northern neighbors. Denationalization decrees were also promulgated by Egypt, Turkey, Austria, and Russia.[25]

In 1933 the Germans issued their denationalization decrees. They were by far the most ominous. They empowered the minister of the interior to cancel naturalizations granted between November 9, 1918 and January 30, 1933. They further provided that all persons of German nationality residing outside of the Reich could be deprived of their citizenship at the discretion of the state.[26] The decree was aimed at Jews and political dissenters. At the time the denationalization decrees were first promulgated, few people dreamed of the ultimate jeopardy to which stateless persons had been condemned by the paper violence of the bureaucrats. In fact, quite a few persons originally claimed that they were stateless as a device to prevent deportation to their native countries, especially when those countries were taken over by hostile regimes. Unfortunately, the Nazis clearly understood the importance of the question of statelessness. When they began to deport Jews from such occupied nations as France, Bulgaria, and Hungary, they insisted that the deportees be stripped of citizenship by their respective governments no later than the day of deportation. There was no need to denationalize Polish and Russian Jews because the Nazis had destroyed the state apparatus as soon as they occupied the territory. The absence of a state apparatus in Poland and occupied Russia was an indication of the ultimate fate of the Poles and the Russians had the Germans won.

In the case of the German Jews, the Nazis used a very simple bureaucratic device to strip them of citizenship. On November 25, 1941 the Reich Citizenship Law was amended to provide that a Jew "who takes up residence abroad" was no longer a Reich national.[27] The property of such persons was to be confiscated by the state. Thus, as soon as the SS transported Jews beyond the German border, no matter how unwilling the Jews were to be "transported," they lost all rights as German nationals. No government anywhere was concerned with what happened to them. The last legal impediment to dealing with them in any fashion the German government elected had been removed.

Men without political rights are superfluous men. They have lost all right to life and human dignity. Political rights are neither God-given, autonomous nor self-validating. The Germans understood that no person has any rights unless they are guaranteed by an organized community with the power to defend such rights. They were perfectly consistent in demanding that the deportees be made stateless before being transported to the camps. They also understood that *by exterminating stateless men and women, they violated no law because such people were covered by no law.* Even those who were committed by religious faith to belief in natural law, such as the hierarchy of the Roman Catholic church, did not see fit to challenge the Nazi actions publicly at the time.

Once the Germans had collected the stateless, rightless, politically superfluous Jews, they exercised a domination over them more total than was ever before exercised in history by one people over another. In the past, political or social domination was limited by the ruler's or the slaveholder's need to permit at least a minimal level of subsistence for his charges. The dominated almost always had some economic value for their masters. Until the twentieth-century camps, there were few situations in which masses of dominated men and women were as good as dead, cut off from the land of the living, and, at the same time, of no long-term use to their masters. Furthermore, the SS knew that in occupied, overpopulated Europe the supply of superfluous, totally dominated people was almost inexhaustible. All that was required, should the supply of Jews be depleted, was the setting apart of other categories of men and women to be condemned to the camps. There is abundant evidence that such indeed was the intention of the Germans. Hilberg quotes a letter written by Otto Thierack, the German minister of justice, on October 13, 1942:

With a view to freeing the German people of Poles, Russians, Jews and Gypsies, and with a view to making the eastern territories which have been incorporated into the Reich available for settlement by German nationals, I intend to turn over criminal jurisdiction over Poles, Russians, Jews and Gypsies to the *Reichsführer-SS* (Himmler). In so doing, I stand on the principle that the administration of justice can make only a small contribution to the extermination of these peoples.[28]

The minister of justice regarded the concentration camps as a place in which to execute such policies for which the normal judicial procedures could make "only a small contribution." He also understood that the scope of the extermination policy was not to be restricted to Jews.

For the first time in history, a ruling elite in the heart of Europe, the center of Western civilization, had an almost inexhaustible supply of men and women with whom they could do anything they pleased, irrespective of any antique religious or moral prejudice. The Nazis had created a society of total domination. Among the preconditions for such a society are: (a) a bureaucratic administration capable of governing with utter indifference to the human needs of the inmates; (b) a supply of inmates capable of continuous replenishment; (c) the imposition of the death sentence on every inmate as soon as he or she enters. Unless the supply is more or less inexhaustible, the masters will be tempted to moderate their treatment of the inmates because of their labor value. If the supply is capable of replenishment, the masters can calculate the exact rate at which they wish to work the prisoners before disposing of them. Both use and riddance can be calculated in terms of the masters' requirements, with only minimal concern for the survival requirements of the slaves. Furthermore, there must be no hope that any inmate might eventually return to normal life. Total domination cannot be achieved if camp guards are apprehensive that some of the inmates might be persons to be reckoned with at some future time. Such cautionary calculation could inhibit the extremities of behavior the camp personnel might otherwise indulge in. The Germans were able to create a society of total domination because of the competence of their police and civil service bureaucracies and because they possessed millions of totally superfluous men whose lives and sufferings were of absolutely no consequence to any power secular or sacred and who were as good as dead the moment they entered the camps.

CHAPTER 3

The Modernization of Slavery

The new form of human order created by the Germans, the society of total domination, was not entirely novel. It was the end product of a long process of political and cultural development. In order to understand the camps as a perfected system of total domination, it is helpful to consider earlier slave societies, especially those in North and South America. As we shall see, these societies only partially anticipate the Nazi universe because of their failure to eliminate all human involvement between the rulers and the ruled. Without the complete depersonalization of human relationships, which Weber identified as the "specific nature" and "special virtue" of bureaucracy, it is impossible to create a true society of total domination.

Devoid of all religious and moral prejudice, a slave is an animated tool. Cotton Mather referred to slaves as "the Animate, Separate, Active Instruments of other men."[1] Wherever the processes of secularization and rationalization are well advanced, no prejudice concerning the slave's humanity will be permitted to interfere with the slave's instrumental character. In recent years, there has been a debate among historians concerning the question of whether slavery was a harsher institution in Protestant North America than in Catholic South America. Both Frank Tannenbaum and Stanley Elkins have argued that in South America slavery was a patriarchal, semifeudal institution which recognized the slave's basic humanity and accorded him a minimum of human rights.[2] Elkins stressed the role of the Roman Catholic church in limiting the slaveowner's power by insisting upon the inviolable character of marriage for all Catholics, whether free or slave.[3] Elkins argued that there were further limitations placed upon the master's right of ownership in Latin America because of the ultimacy of royal power.[4] Another element that mitigated the harshness of the slave's condition was the fact that law in Latin America derived from Roman law which presupposed the fundamental *inequality* of all men. By contrast, North American law proclaimed that all men are created equal, but then had the gravest difficulty in dealing with the humanity of those who were obviously unequal. In North America state-imposed restrictions on the slaveowner's property were minimal. Furthermore, the social attitudes of the Southern Protestant churches usually reflected the interests of the dominant slaveowning class, upon whom the clergy were financially dependent. By contrast, in Latin America, the Roman Catholic hierarchy was somewhat independent of the owning classes.[5] In addition, according to Elkins, the tendency of capitalism to rationalize labor relations and reduce them to money relations was much more advanced in the plantations of North America than in Latin America.[6]

David Brion Davis has challenged the Tannenbaum-Elkins thesis, arguing that some of the worst instances of ill-treatment of slaves were to be found in the mines of Catholic Brazil and that Elkins neglected much of the evidence demonstrating the extent to which attempts were made to mitigate the worst features of slavery in North America. Yet, in spite of his disagreement with Elkins, Davis finds that "slavery in Latin America, compared with that in North America, was less subject to the pressures of competitive capitalism and was closer to a system of patriarchal rights and semifeudalistic services."[7] Both Davis and Elkins are in agreement on two fundamental points: (a) Overall, slavery was far more subject to the pressures of a competitive, impersonal capitalist system in North America; (b) In both North and South America, wherever slavery was linked to capitalist rather than semifeudal enterprise, it tended to be far less humane. Wherever slavery was employed in enterprise based upon the requirements of a money economy, the age-old contradiction in the nature of slavery, the fact that a slave is a human being who is regarded as a thing, was resolved by emphasizing the slave's thinglike quality and deemphasizing his humanity.[8]

From the moment the slave was shipped as commercial cargo across the Atlantic in the infamous "Middle Passage," and sold as an animated tool with a legal status often no different than that of a domesticated animal, he was a creature devoid of all effective legal and political status. He ceased to be a human being in law, save where his human status was of advantage to his master. Where laws were placed on the books protecting the slave from violent abuse, such laws offered little realistic protection. The slave's testimony was never accepted against a white man's, especially by a jury of the white man's peers.[9]

The parallels between the treatment of the slaves in transit from Africa to the New World and the death-camp inmates are unhappily instructive. According to Elkins, the process by which the slaves were transported from Africa to the Caribbean, where they were stripped, deprived of name, identity, and language, and then sold as chattel at auction in the United States, anticipated the process by which the Nazis shipped their victims in overcrowded freight trains, compelled them to strip, exchanged their names for numbers and then either incarcerated them as slave labor or murdered them outright.[10] The sea journey of the slave ships was a horror comparable only to the German freight cars. The same calculating rationality that was to figure in the work of the German bureaucrats was already at work in the New England and British sea captains who transported the sorrowful cargo. In all, it has been estimated that over fifteen million people were transported from Africa to the Americas during the slave-trade period.[11] Every day the corpses of those who had perished the previous night, a precisely calculable attrition of cargo, were tossed overboard. And, some very respectable New England fortunes were made in those ventures.

Yet, there were important differences between the slaves and the camp inmates. The Jewish deportees were people whom nobody wanted and who were to be found on a continent one of whose most urgent problems was to get rid of people. In spite of World War I and the subsequent civil wars, as well as the loss of people through emigration, Europe in the thirties had more people than it needed, given its political and economic structure. The Germans were interested in accelerating the rate of population reduction, at least for their subject peoples. By contrast, there was a population shortage in antebellum North America, and, with, the cessation of the slave trade, slaves had to be bred rather than imported. As evidence of the relatively mild treatment of slaves in North America, apologists for the system have pointed out that the South had the only slave population in the New World that successfully reproduced itself. In all, about four hundred thousand slaves had been imported into the British-American colonies and the United States; by 1860 there were about four million slaves in the South.[12] Slaves are far better treated when their masters seek to augment their numbers through reproduction than when they are deliberately worked to death, as they were during World War II.

In the nineteenth century there was a continent to be won. Free white settlers would not and could not provide the labor necessary for all the tasks at hand. The imported slaves may have lacked political rights, but they did possess a measure of economic value and the feelings of a valued slave could not be entirely ignored. There were, of course, many instances of gratuitous cruelty on the part of slaveholders and their overseers. Nevertheless, there was a tendency, especially after 1831, to mitigate many of the worst features of harsh treatment. As Eugene D. Genovese has pointed out, the plantation system in the South was paternalistic and this paternalism had the effect of limiting the extent to which masters could dominate their slaves.[13] Although racial and cultural differences intensified barriers, human relations did develop between masters and slaves. In addition, in many communities unduly cruel masters were often ostracized by their peers.[14]

Furthermore, there is a growing consensus among students of slavery that the *material* conditions of slaves in North America did not compare unfavorably with those of unskilled "free" workers in Europe's industrial centers in the first half of the nineteenth century.[15] It can be argued that North American slavery was precapitalist since there was no precise method of calculation by which a slaveowner might estimate his labor costs. As long as a master was obliged to maintain his slaves in season and out, in good times and bad, his operation could not be considered fully rationalized and, hence, capitalist. Thus, one of the consequences of the Civil War was the enforced extension of rationalized, impersonal labor relations to all sections of the United States. It can also be argued that the transformation of the national pool of slave labor into nominally free, mobile, wage labor was an indispensable step in the process of the rationalization of labor relations. It is, for example, far more rational for a giant agribusiness corporation to hire itinerant wage labor as needed than it was for a slaveowner to attempt a comparable operation with a relatively permanent slave-labor force. Thus, contemporary agricultural and industrial operations that rely upon mobile wage labor represent a genuine "advance" in both rationalization and depersonalization over the older, less efficient slave system. The greater "rationality" and calculability of "free" labor in a money economy over slave labor has been stated succinctly by Jürgen Kuczynski: "One usually looks after property (slaves) better than 'things' (free workers) which belong to no one and which one can use so long as they are serviceable, and then throw out on the street."[16] As we shall see, the final step in the rationalization of labor relations was taken in World War II by the great German business corporations that invested huge sums in the construction of factories at death camps for the express purpose of utilizing the available and infinitely replenishable pool of death-camp slave labor. The employer's responsibility for the maintenance of the work force was reduced to an absolute minimum, the subsistence requirements necessary to keep a worker alive for a precisely calculated period of weeks or months. The whole enterprise was further rationalized by the fact that one no longer needed to turn used-up laborers "out on the street" where they could become a source of infectious social pathology. It was both more practical and more economical simply to incinerate them.

Slavery in North America was thus an imperfectly rationalized institution of nearly total domination under conditions of a *shortage of productive labor*. The death camp was a fully rationalized institution of total domination under conditions of a *population surplus*. In the German camps, the inmates had neither political status nor long-term economic value. There was, admittedly, a temporary wartime labor shortage and both the *Wehrmacht* and a number of German corporations sought to secure the exemption of their skilled Jewish laborers from deportation. However, the motive of economic utility was never strong enough to overrule the decision to kill the Jews. Himmler was constantly being asked to exempt certain categories of Jews because of their usefulness to war production. In every instance, the exemptions, when granted, were only temporary.[17] In all likelihood, many of the temporary exemptions were granted to delude Jews into thinking that it was possible to save themselves by strict obedience. The exemptions never lasted. In terms of long-term German priorities, Jewish labor had no value. To argue that the Jews could have been used productively is beside the point. Even the pragmatic calculations that motivated slaveowners to treat their slaves with some measure of humanity were totally absent.

According to David Brion Davis, it is impossible to understand slavery as an institution if one overlooks "certain continuities and common features in the history of servitude." Yet, even Davis admits that

No slave system in history was quite like that of the West Indies and the Southern states of America. Marked off from the free population by racial and cultural differences, for the most part deprived of the hope of manumission, the Negro slave also found life regimented in a highly organized system that was geared to a market economy.[18]

While no slave system was like that of North America, the American system can be seen as a link in the process of the progressive rationalization of a system of total domination that reached its full development in the Nazi camps. Just as there is historic continuity between the North American slave system and its predecessors, so too there is continuity between the Nazi system and *both* the earlier slave systems and the impersonal use of "free" labor in a money economy. Furthermore, it is significant that (a) the most systematic and methodical version of slavery was established in Protestant and capitalist North America, and (b) the most systematic, dehumanized form of exploitation of "free" labor was established by the "self-made parvenus" of Protestant, nonconformist and capitalist Manchester, England. Here too, there is continuity with the death and slave-labor camps.[18a] The same tendencies towards rationalization, secularization, and disenchantment that are expressed in both Protestantism and capitalism are also expressed with far less ambiguity and contradiction in the Nazi camps. It is, however, as little my intention to suggest that Protestantism was responsible for the forms that the exploitation of free and slave labor took in nineteenth-century England and America as it was my intention to suggest that Protestantism was to blame for the Nazi camps. It must not be forgotten that the abolitionist movement was also a direct expression of the religious and moral commitments of Protestants. Yet, it can with justice be asserted that the rationalized forms of exploitation of both free and slave labor were among the unanticipated sociological consequences of the secularization and rationalization processes that are biblical in origin and which were developed more consistently in Protestantism than elsewhere.

North American slaves were among the first group of human beings who lacked all effective legal and political rights and who were forcibly detained in areas of concentration in a country that regarded itself as an heir of the religious and cultural traditions of the Western world. Those plantations in which slave labor was regimented and systematized in the interests of a money economy anticipated the modern concentration camp, although it must be repeated that, save for the dehumanizing process whereby Africans were captured, transported, and transformed psychologically into slaves, there can be little comparison between the treatment of North American slaves and that of the camp inmates. That, however, is not the fundamental issue. The institution of slavery in America is further evidence that the death camps were the end product of a very long cultural and political development involving all of the major countries of the Western world, rather than the specialized and extraordinary hatred of the Germans for the Jews. On the contrary, taken together, the record of the British, Portugese, Dutch, French, and Spanish in Africa, Asia, and the Americas is quantitatively as blood-stained as that of the Germans.[19] The Germans were, however, late-comers to the twin games of slavery and slaughter, but they utilized advanced methods to do more efficiently in the heart of Europe what other Europeans did elsewhere.

As we have seen, the slaves were protected by more or less precise calculation of the sort of treatment that was likely to result in the best use of their labor. There were, of course, exceptions. According to Davis, planters in both Brazil and the West Indies had little incentive to improve working conditions or to limit the hours of work. The life expectancy of their slaves was no more than a few years and they could be cheaply replaced.[20] Under such circumstances, the lives of slaves were of little value. In North America, the slaves were an important part of the slave owners' capital. However, the value of capital assets tends to fluctuate. This was true of the slaves. In the 1850s one of the most crucial economic problems confronting the slave owners in the older slaveholding states such as Virginia was a growing slave surplus. Although the slaves had to be fed, clothed, and housed, in many places there were more of them than were required for the available work. Eugene Genovese has argued that one of the reasons for the South's interest in opening up the newer territories in the West to slavery was that new slave states would provide a market where surplus slaves might be sold.[21] There was a point beyond which the possession of slaves ceased to be profitable. There were also strong legal barriers against the manumission of slaves, largely because of racial sentiments.[22] Were a plantation compelled to feed and house more slaves than it could profitably employ, the owner might eventually go bankrupt. As long as there were territories that could absorb the excess, slaves represented an asset. They could, however, easily become a liability were there no market for them.

Such a problem would not have troubled the Nazis. We have seen that they had a simple way of disposing of surplus people. Had the Nazis managed the Southern plantations they would have regarded the slaves as *Tiermenschen*, subhuman, (literally, "animal men") and granted the surplus slaves a "mercy death." While the law in most slave states tended to classify the sale and possession of slaves with the sale and possession of cattle, Southern slave owners were not at liberty to dispose of excess, unprofitable slaves in the same manner as excess, unprofitable cattle. That improvement in labor economics had to await the twentieth century. Superannuated slaves were permitted to live out their days; idiots were not relegated to euthenasia programs.

The sexual relations of masters and slaves have frequently been noted. Lacking all rights, female slaves were always subject to sexual abuse even when laws protecting women were on the books. Nevertheless, sexual intercourse often became the basis of enduring personal relations on the plantations. Strong bonds of affection often developed. Masters often had two families, an official white and an unofficial black family. From the point of view of strict calculating rationality, such liaisons compromised the dominance of the slave owner. Personal relations often led to human if not legal claims by the slave on the master's resources for herself and her offspring. Although the master was not legally obliged to honor such claims, it was difficult to reject them entirely.[23]

In the Nazi camps, there was a strict policy of discouraging sexual contacts between the SS and the prisoners. Jewish women were, of course, very often sexually abused, but personal relationships were not permitted to develop. At Auschwitz, several brothels were organized in order to minimize the temptation to resort to unauthorized liaisons.[24] Sexual contact with a Jewish woman was in any event regarded as the crime of "racial pollution." From a strictly bureaucratic point of view, sexual relations can threaten the pure objectivity with which a structure of total dominance is maintained. The SS understood that the more depersonalized the relations between the masters and the slaves become, the more effectively the slaves can be utilized.

In the first stages of the destruction process, when the Jews were being rounded up by mobile killing units *(Einsatzgruppen)* and shot to death beside mass graves, there were a number of incidents in which doomed Jewish girls desperately offered themselves to members of SS mobile killing units in the hope of saving themselves. Invariably, the girls were used for the night and then killed the next day.[25] Thus, even in the sphere of sexual abuse, there was a vast difference between the American system of slavery and the Nazi camps. For the great plantations to have become fully rationalized bureaucratic ventures in total domination, all personal relations between masters and slaves would have been prohibited. That step was never taken. If Genovese is correct in his contention that one of the forces making for the Civil War in America was the pressure on the slave owners to expand the territory available for slavery so that there would be a viable market for the sale of slaves, then it is clear that the leaders of the South preferred a bloody war in which they were ultimately defeated to the kind of radical "solution" employed in the twentieth century. No matter how far the processes of rationalization and secularization had proceeded in the antebellum South, no matter how devoid of rights the slaves may have been, no matter how calculating the master, he remained a paternalistic Christian for whom some limits could not yet be breached. Nevertheless, as we have stated, the slave plantations and the concentration camps are part of the same developmental continuum within Western civilization.

We have alluded to a basic contradiction in slavery as an institution: The slave was a human being who was treated as a thing and defined as such in law. Every system of slavery until the twentieth century experienced a certain tension because of the contradiction. The Nazis were the first masters to resolve it. They were able to turn human beings into instruments wholly responsive to their will even when told to lie down in their own graves and be shot. That is perhaps the supreme "achievement" of their society of total domination. Unfortunately, if it is true that every system of domination has an inherent tendency towards the expansion of its power, then the society of total domination may prove to be a permanent temptation to future rulers, especially in stressful times. Every ruler seeks affirmative response to command. As long as a residue of unpredictable freedom of action is possible in his subjects, the ruler's assured response to command escapes him. The Nazis have taught that what cannot be achieved by persuasion or even by a system of rewards can be achieved by terror.

Originally, the SS did not have any interest in utilizing Jews as slave labor in the camps. Several steps were required in the development of the process of destruction before Jews were used in concentration camps as slaves. In the first period, immediately after the German invasion of Russia which began on June 22, 1941, an agreement between the *Wehrmacht* and the SS provided that, as the *Wehrmacht* entered Soviet territory, the SS's *Einsatzgruppen*, the mobile killing units, would, with the full cooperation of the *Wehrmacht*, be permitted to exterminate all Jews in the invaded territories. The means of killing was by shooting at mass graves.[26] However, Himmler and other SS leaders became concerned about the psychological effect of the shooting on the killers. As always, Himmler's concern was organizational not moral. A less problematic means of killing was sought. Finally, the mass gas chamber utilizing Zyklon B was put to use.[27] It had the advantage of the greatest capacity with the fewest undesirable effects on the SS personnel.

By the beginning of 1941, the SS was the only German institution with a labor surplus, and for obvious reasons. The SS took advantage of the situation. The *Wirtschafts-Verwaltungshauptamt* (WVHA), the SS Economic-Administrative Main Office, was established under the direction of Oswald Pohl to take charge of slave-labor programs in the camps.[28] The death-camp system became a society of total domination only when healthy inmates were kept alive and forced to become slaves rather than killed outright. To repeat, as long as the camps served the single function of killing prisoners, one can speak of the camps as places of mass execution but not as a new type of human society. Most of the literature on the camps has tended to stress the role of the camps as places of execution. Regrettably, few ethical theorists or religious thinkers have paid attention to the highly significant political fact that the camps were in reality a new form of human society.

Only when the doomed inmates were kept alive for a time did the new society develop. It was at Auschwitz that the most effective system of extermination, mass gas chambers using Zyklon B coupled with on-the-spot mass crematoria, was first put to use. It was also at Auschwitz that the most thoroughgoing society of total domination in human history was established. Much has been written about the infamous Dr. Joseph Mengele, the physician at Auschwitz, who used to meet the new arrivals and separate those who were to be killed immediately from those who were to be worked to death as slaves. Such a selection process did not take place at camps like Treblinka because they functioned only as killing centers. At Auschwitz, the camp served two seemingly contradictory purposes: Auschwitz was both a slave-labor and an execution center. Yet, these purposes were not really contradictory. Given the nature of slavery as practiced by the Germans, only doomed slaves could successfully be dealt with as things rather than as human beings.

CHAPTER 4

The Health Professions and
Corporate Enterprise
at Auschwitz

In a society of total domination, there is absolutely no moral limit on the uses normal, perverse, or obscene to which the masters can put the human beings at their disposal. We have noted that this included extreme sexual abuse as well as enforced slavery. Before discussing slave labor at Auschwitz, let us consider another use of the prisoners, their utilization as human guinea pigs in the Nazi medical experiments. From the point of view of pragmatic rationality, devoid of religious or moral sentimentality, human beings are often the most suitable subjects for medical experiments. Dogs, guinea pigs, and monkeys are only partially acceptable surrogates. In non-Nazi societies, men and women, often prisoners, have on occasion volunteered to participate in medical experiments in return for compensation such as a shortened prison term. In a society of total domination, no such compensation is needed.

Once German physicians realized that they had an almost limitless supply of human beings at their disposal for experiments, some very respectable professors at medical schools and research institutes seized the unique opportunity. Their findings were reported at meetings of medical societies. On no occasion was any protest recorded.[1] Perhaps the most extreme example of the use of the medical profession to transform human beings into things took place at the instigation of Professor Hirt who was the director of anatomical research at the Reich University in Strasbourg. Hirt was also a *Hauptsturmführer* in the SS. Early in 1942 Hirt wrote to Himmler informing him that all nations and races had been studied by means of skull collections save the Jews. He pointed out that the war in the East offered an opportunity to correct the deficiency: "In the Jewish-Bolshevist commissars, who embody a repulsive but characteristic subhumanity, we have the possibility of obtaining a plastic source for scientific study if we secure their skulls."[2] In order that the anatomical specimens be in optimum condition, Hirt advised that the Jews be kept alive until a doctor could take down accurate statistics. They were then to be killed and their heads removed with proper scientific care. After some delay, one of Dr. Hirt's colleagues, Dr. Bruno Begor, was sent to Auschwitz where he selected seventy-nine Jewish men, thirty Jewish women, four central Asians and two Poles. Those chosen were gassed and their bodies were brought to Strasbourg where they were used for racial studies. The whole enterprise was sponsored by *Ahenerbe*, a society founded by the SS in 1939 to study "the sphere, spirit, deed and heritage of the Nordic Indo-Germanic race."[3] Its president was Himmler.

In addition to an ideological interest in the achievements of the "Nordic Indo-Germanic race," the leadership of the SS encouraged experiments whose aim was to discover an economical and efficient means of sterilizing large populations. The Germans had several purposes in mind in carrying out sterilization experiments. One was the sticky problem of what to do with the *Mischlinge*, persons of part German, part Jewish descent.[4] When the distinctions between Jews and Aryans were first worked out in the early years of the regime, the Nazi directives provided for greater disabilities for those with the most Jewish "blood" and/or the greatest involvement with Judaism and the Jewish community. Those with the least Jewish blood, who had married Christians and had been baptized, were treated with the greatest leniency. Nevertheless, every *Mischling* introduced some Jewish blood into the otherwise pure German bloodstream. There was a great deal of discussion of what might be done with the *Mischlinge*, especially *Mischlinge* of "the first degree," those with most Jewish blood. By October 27, 1942, when a conference on the *Mischlinge* was held with Adolf Eichmann as chairman, it was agreed that such *Mischlinge* be sterilized immediately. Sterilization was to be considered a voluntary act to which the *Mischlinge* consented because they had "graciously" been permitted to live on Reich territory.[5] The *Mischlinge* were to be permitted to live out their lives without "defiling" German blood.

The decision to sterilize the *Mischlinge* was based upon the mistaken premise that the doctors who were conducting the experiments in the camps had achieved a breakthrough in their search for an efficient form of mass sterilization. In reality, there was no such breakthrough.

The sterilization experiments were initiated as a result of correspondence between Adolf Pokorny, a retired Army doctor, and Himmler.[6] Pokorny wrote to Himmler about an article in a medical journal describing the effect of injecting the extract of a plant, *Caladium seguinum* into rodents. Sterilization ensued. He proposed that the plant be produced on a large scale and that experiments be initiated to determine whether it could be used on human beings. He pointedly referred to the three million Russian prisoners of war in German hands. Pokorny's letter suggested to Himmler the possibility of perfecting a method of mass sterilization that could result in the ultimate elimination of *any* group the Nazis might designate as "inferior." Because of the availability of prisoners, an "experimental block" was set up at Auschwitz and sterilization experiments were begun under the direction of Professor Carl Clauberg, chief physician of the womens' clinic at a hospital in Konigshütte, Upper Silesia. He proposed that an irritant be placed in the uterus of female prisoners by means of a syringe. He made use of the virtually unlimited supply of subjects available for his experiments. He told his victims that they were being artificially inseminated. He then injected the irritant. It was his hope to perfect his process so that a single doctor with ten paramedical assistants could sterilize a thousand women a day on a more or less assembly line basis. Clauberg failed to "perfect" his system although he kept writing enthusiastic reports claiming that he was on the brink of success.[7]

There were other attempts to achieve the evasive breakthrough. Some involved outright castration and surgical mutilation of the uterus. Hilberg cites a letter written in March 1941 by Viktor Brack of the Führer Chancellery in which he proposed that sterilization take place by the simple means of compelling "the persons to be processed" to step up to a counter and fill out some forms. While the forms were being filled out, a German bureaucrat behind the counter would turn on an X-ray machine capable of sterilizing the unsuspecting victim. From a bureaucratic point of view, this was the "cleanest" method of sterilization. Brack also forwarded cost estimates involved in setting up twenty counters at which three to four thousand people could be sterilized daily.[8]

When Brack first made his proposal, Himmler did not seem very interested. A year later Brack reminded Himmler of the X-ray proposal at a time when there was some discussion of using three million of the estimated ten million doomed Jews for slave-labor purposes. Brack proposed that the slaves be sterilized to prevent their reproduction while they were kept alive as workers. Himmler decided that there was sufficient merit in Brack's proposal to warrant the initiation of experiments at Auschwitz to test the feasibility of mass X-ray sterilization. Hundreds of prisoners were used in the experiments. Many died, but, again, the sterilization experiments failed to produce a satisfactory result. Those in charge finally came to the conclusion that surgical castration was speedier and more efficient.

Hilberg divides the medical experiments into two general categories: those utilizing the available supply of prisoners to conduct tests that would have been normal attempts to extend medical knowledge had the subjects participated willingly, and those whose purpose was to discover a means whereby the Germans could rule Europe forever.[9] The sterilization experiments were clearly in the latter category. And the death camps were the logical place in which to conduct them. The experiments were part of the same war of extermination against non-Germans that was being carried out in the gas chambers. Nor ought we to lose sight of the logic of what the Germans were up to. If one wishes security against real or imagined enemies, it is not enough to defeat them in war. A defeated enemy may some day rise again and seek vengeance. Total security can only be achieved by biological means. The enemy must either be killed or sterilized. And, no antique Christian prejudice must be permitted to interfere.

As we have noted, had the Germans won the war, mass sterilization would have been an important aspect of their program for the subject peoples. *It must be remembered that with both the Nazis and the Bolsheviks, victory inevitably led to an intensification rather than a diminution of terror.* Mass sterilization of Poles, Russians and, in the more distant future, the French and the Italians, would have permitted the Germans to exploit the vanquished at their own convenience in the certain knowledge that the subject peoples' national existence was at an end. Whether extermination or killing was the means of securing absolute dominance or whether a certain number of the vanquished might be permitted to reproduce in exactly calculable quantities would have depended solely on the requirements of the German masters. The victims would have had as little control over their own destiny as cattle in a stockyard. In a society of total domination, helots could be killed, bred, or sterilized at will.

Nevertheless, it would be a mistake to see the medical experiments as the outcome of some special viciousness of which only German doctors are capable. The Germans have no monopoly on the kind of mentality that would utilize powerless human beings as unwilling or unsuspecting subjects of such experiments. Recently, it became known that a group of black prisoners suffering from syphilis in an American prison were divided into two groups, one of which was given medication to cure or control the disease, the other was given a placebo. The object of the experiment was to compare the effects of medication with that of letting the disease run its course. The organizers of the experiment had cold-bloodedly condemned the prisoners who received the placebo to the mutilating effects of disease and/or death in the name of scientific rationality. The experiment that did come to light was different from the Nazi experiments only in that the American prisoners were completely unaware of what was being done to them. Most of the Nazi victims had some idea of what was happening. The same "modern" mentality that gives a higher priority to solving an administratively defined problem than to its effect on human beings characterized both the American and the German experiments.

Furthermore, the practice of using prisoner "volunteers" for medical experiments is currently very widespread in the United States. According to Jessica Mitford, one reputable American scientist was reputed to have said, "Criminals in our penitentiaries are fine experimental material—and much cheaper than chimpanzees." According to the Food and Drug Administration, as of 1973, such experiments were being carried on in about fifty prisons in twenty-four states. Prisoners are usually "paid" one dollar a day for their participation. Unfortunately, there is much permanent damage to the "volunteers" and even loss of life. During World War II, the great German pharmaceutical corporation, Bayer A. G. of Leverkusen, made extensive use of death-camp inmates for their experiments on human beings. Today, Bayer's American corporate counterparts, such as Lederle, Bristol-Myers, Squibb, Merck, Sharp and Dohme, and Upjohn, have found a plentiful supply of subjects (objects?) in America's prisons for their "voluntary" experiments on human beings. The experiments in American prisons have the cooperation and the approval of such federal bureaucracies as the Department of Health, Education and Welfare and the Food and Drug Administration. Ms. Mitford quotes Dr. Sheldon Margen, a physician opposed to the experiments, as saying,

If the researchers really believe these experiments are safe for humans, why do they go to the prisons for the subjects? Why don't they try them out in their own labs on students? . . . Because they know the university would never permit this. . . . They make a distinction between people they think of as social equals or colleagues and men behind bars, whom they regard as less than human.[10]

Nor is it accidental that the American doctors selected blacks as their subjects in the syphilis experiments. The blacks are the American equivalent of the Nazi *Tiermenschen*, subhumans, concerning whom no effective protest was anticipated. It is likely that racism is indispensable to a society of total domination. Certainly, racism facilitates the ascription of paranthropoid identity to human beings. Once the victim is categorized as belonging to a different species, the task of transforming him into a thing is immensely simplified. Undoubtedly, the harsh forms of slavery that characterized the ante-bellum South were facilitated by the fact that the blacks were different in both race and culture from their masters.[11] Before the Nazis assaulted the Jews, the Poles, the Russians, and the Gypsies, they were categorized as members of sub-human races.

Another recent American parallel to the Nazi experiments was the decision of welfare authorities in Georgia to sterilize several mentally deficient black girls. Their illiterate parents were allegedly compelled by representatives of the welfare bureaucracy to sign papers permitting the sterilization.[12] The syphilis experiments and the sterilization of the black girls are in all likelihood but the tip of the iceberg.

As we have noted, one of the German institutions that recognized the potentialities of total domination was the Bayer chemical division of the giant I. G. Farben cartel. I. G. Farben was involved in both medical experiments and slave labor utilization at Auschwitz. Before its enforced dissolution at the end of the war, I. G. Farben was a huge chemical and pharmaceutical conglomerate, whose corporate subsidiaries included the Bayer aspirin and the Agfa film concerns. The Bayer research laboratories were interested in testing an antityphus medicine that had been prepared in both tablet and powder form. Some patients threw up when given the tablets. Bayer wanted to ascertain whether the powder or the tablets had the fewest side effects. At first, the Bayer researchers approached a "friendly insane asylum" and were granted permission to test the medicine on some of the patients. The experiments failed because of the inability of the mentally ill patients to distinguish between the powder and the pills. As luck would have it, one of I. G. Farben's research workers was serving as *Obersturmbahnführer* at Auschwitz. His help was enlisted and Bayer was permitted to conduct its experiments on camp inmates.[13]

Bayer's experiments were relatively innocent. This was not true of most of I. G. Farben's corporate activities at Auschwitz. I. G. Farben was the most important German corporate employer of slave labor at Auschwitz. The corporation's activities at Auschwitz are an important part of the story of the camp as a society of total domination. In the nineteenth century, Karl Marx and Friedrich Engels had observed that the economic triumph of the bourgeoisie, the class of modern capitalists that owned the "means of production", had "left remaining no other nexus between man and man than naked self-interest, than callous cash payment."[14] Marx and Engels were pointing to the same process of "dehumanized" rationalization as had Weber, who regarded the large corporation as a type of bureaucratic organization that rivaled the state bureaucracy in achieving rational efficiency and calculated results.[15] According to Marx, the bourgeoisie had reduced industrial labor to a commodity "like every other article of commerce."[16] Marx claimed that in capitalist enterprise the cost of labor was restricted to the "means of subsistence" required by the laborer "for his maintenance and the propagation of the race."[17] In view of the conditions of the working class in England, Europe's most industrialized nation in the 1840s, the observations were more than justified. As uprooted men and women were forced to move from the countryside to the cities, they had little choice but to accept the subsistence wages offered to them in the mills and factories. The alternative was starvation. There was an abundant labor supply and its cost was kept at a minimum.[18] Unlike the old feudal order, the relations between the mill and mine workers and their employers were totally impersonal. The workers were unsentimentally regarded as a necessary component in the production mechanism, but each worker was seen as an interchangeable, easily replaceable unit in a depersonalized mechanism that was calculated solely in terms of minimum costs and maximum profits.

The bourgeois order, especially in England, produced a system of exploitation of free labor unparalleled for its cruelty in all of human history. The abusive use of women and children and the utter indifference to the health and well-being of the workers were a normal part of the system. There is no more fitting term with which to describe those wretched men and women than wage slaves. In Victorian England, the wage slaves had become servo-mechanisms of the machines they tended. As Marx has observed, "as machines become more human, men become more like machines."[19]

As soon as profit and productivity became the sole criteria by which a business enterprise was to be measured, it was in the factory owner's interest to work his employees as long as he could and pay them as little as he could get away with. As we know, this kind of exploitation did not last in England or on the continent. For exploitation to be truly systematic, there must be a pool of *unorganized individuals* who are confronted singly with the alternatives of becoming wage slaves or starving. The workers of England and the continent were ultimately able to defend themselves politically and economically by securing the right to vote and by organizing trade unions.[20] In the ghettoes and concentration camps run by the Germans, it was impossible for individuals to oppose the system and, save for the last days of the Warsaw ghetto, those Jewish organizations that might have become the foci of resistance were controlled by the Germans. To the extent that it is today possible to speak of the "dignity of labor," it is because labor acquired the indispensable precondition of any kind of human dignity, organizational strength, and through that strength, a measure of power. Had labor been unable to organize, it is not likely that the conditions of the working classes would have improved greatly. It is more likely that labor would have been treated as the commodity Marx said it was under capitalism. When there is an oversupply of any commodity under free market conditions, its cost tends to drop. The price of labor would have fluctuated with its relative scarcity or abundance, irrespective of the human or even the subsistence needs of the workers. In a purely rationalized system of production, as Marx understood, the human element in labor can and ought to be ignored.

One of the reasons for the failure of Marx's prophecy that the working class in capitalist countries would in desperation be driven to revolution was that it was never possible for bourgeois society totally to reduce labor to a commodity. A commodity is inert. It cannot organize and it cannot fight back. Only where men can be reduced to thinglike automatons, capable of fulfilling assigned tasks but incapable of any effective protest on their own behalf, can a perfectly rationalized system of production or domination be achieved. That achievement was not possible for the factory owners of nineteenth-century England because they were neither prepared nor even cognizant of the kinds of political and social transformations that would be required to create so compliant a working force. The Germans were able to create such a force in the death camps.

Some of Germany's largest and most advanced corporations, such as I. G. Farben, seized the opportunity to utilize the camp prisoners as a labor force. In 1933 I. G. Farben was not an anti-Semitic corporation. It employed many Jews. Jews had helped to build the huge corporate empire. A Jew, Dr. Karl von Weinberg, was the deputy chairman of the corporation's *Verwaltungsrat*, its advisory board of corporate elder statesmen. In 1933 after Hitler came to power, von Weinberg continued for a while to function as a member of the corporation's elite. He encouraged a group of visiting American executives from E. I. DuPont du Nemours of Wilmington, Delaware, to increase their collaboration with the German firm. However, as the process of eliminating Jews from German life intensified in the thirties, I. G. Farben naturally got rid of its Jewish officials, although the corporation did try to transfer some Jewish personnel to foreign posts because of their value to the firm. Even this was only a temporary measure.[22]

By 1939 I. G. Farben was fully integrated into the new German order. During the war, it was faced with a severe labor shortage at a time when Germany's military and civilian needs for *Buna*, synthetic rubber, were expanding rapidly. It was decided to build a new plant for the manufacture of synthetic rubber. I. G. Farben officials met with officials of the Economy Ministry to decide on the location of the new factory. After several meetings, the corporation executives were convinced by the Economy Ministry officials of the advantages of constructing several plants at Auschwitz. The Auschwitz site had good supplies of water, coal, and other needed ingredients. The problem of an assured labor supply was solved by Himmler who promised that all available skilled workers held at Auschwitz would be placed at the giant corporation's disposal. This took place on February 6, 1941.[22] I. G. Farben's decision to locate at Auschwitz was based upon the very same criteria by which contemporary multinational corporations relocate their plants in utter indifference to the social consequences of such moves: wherever possible costs, especially labor costs, must be minimized and profits maximized. In February 1941, Auschwitz appeared to be an excellent corporate investment to some of Germany's most respectable business leaders. Their mentality was not very different from that of corporate executives who close down plants in such high labor cost areas as Stuttgart and Philadelphia and relocate them in Manila and Singapore. This should occasion neither surprise nor shock. I. G. Farben was one of the first great corporate conglomerates. Its executives merely carried the logic of corporate rationality to its ultimate conclusion. As we have observed, the perfect labor force for a corporation that seeks fully to minimize costs and maximize profits is slave labor in a death camp. Among the great German corporations who utilized slave labor were AEG (German General Electric), Wanderer-Autounion (Audi), Krupp, Rheinmetall Borsig, Siemens-Schuckert and Telefunken.[23]

I. G. Farben's investment in I. G. Auschwitz ultimately reached 700,000,000 Reichsmark. This is over $1,000,000,000 in today's money. The construction work required 170 contractors. Two company villages were built to house corporate personnel. Barracks were, of course, built for the inmates. When the factories commenced operations, the SS provided guards to supervise the workers. When rules were violated, the SS administered punishment according to their normal procedures.[24]

The diet of the inmates was the same starvation diet of watery turnip soup given to all Auschwitz inmates, save that the corporation added a ration of extra *"Buna* soup," not out of consideration for the workers' well-being but to maintain a precisely calculated level of productivity.[25] Marx had written that the level of compensation in capitalist industrial enterprise had to be sufficient to maintain a minimal level of subsistence. At I. G. Auschwitz there was no reason to tax the corporation's resources even to that extent. Given the almost inexhaustible supply of labor, the company adopted a deliberate policy of working slaves to death. Nor was the policy hidden from the top echelons of I. G. Farben's managerial elite. They were very much involved in the operation and made frequent trips to Auschwitz to see how things were going. According to the affidavit of Dr. Raymond van den Straaten, a slave at Auschwitz, on one occasion, five of I. G. Farben's top directors made an inspection tour of I. G. Auschwitz. As one of the directors passed a slave scientist, Dr. Fritz Lohner-Beda, the Director remarked, "The Jewish swine could work a little faster." Another I. G. Farben director responded, "If they don't work, let them perish in the gas chamber." Dr. Lohner-Beda was then pulled out of his group and kicked to death.[26]

One of the five directors present on that occasion was Dr. Fritz Ter Meer, I. G. Farben's executive in charge of synthetic rubber and petrochemical operations including I. G. Auschwitz. As a top I. G. Farben executive, Dr. Ter Meer visited the United States on a number of occasions before America's entry into World War II. He had excellent relations with his American corporate counterparts, especially Mr. Frank Howard, chief executive officer of Standard Oil of New Jersey, as well as other top Standard Oil executives. (Jersey Standard has been incorporated into the Exxon Corporation). An important objective of Dr. Ter Meer's American trips was to conclude a series of cartel agreements with Standard Oil for the ostensible purpose of dividing up the world market for the manufacture and distribution of synthetic rubber or Buna between I. G. Farben and Jersey Standard. Dr. Ter Meer's real objective was to cripple American production of synthetic rubber in case of war by making Standard Oil dependent upon I. G. Farben's contracts, patents and licenses. He succeeded so well that for months after the attack on Pearl Harbor, Standard Oil honored its cartel agreements with the enemy corporation. This had the effect of depriving America of urgently needed synthetic rubber at a time when the normal sources of natural rubber in Southeast Asia had been cut off by the Japanese.

Deprived of natural rubber by the Japanese and synthetic rubber by Standard Oil's refusal to permit even the war to interfere with its business arrangements, the Federal government was initially unsuccessful in its efforts to get Standard Oil to break its cartel agreements with the enemy corporation. Had a private individual behaved as did this great corporation, it is very likely that he would have been suspected of profound disloyalty if not outright treason.[27]

Dr. Ter Meer was equally at home as the executive officer responsible for I. G. Auschwitz and as an honored and respected corporate colleague of some of the most important business executives in the United States in the late thirties and early forties. Nor did Dr. Ter Meer express any regret about I. G. Auschwitz after the war. When queried by a British officer, Major Edmund Tilley, whether he regretted the experiments conducted upon concentration camp victims by I. G. Farben's pharmaceutical subsidiaries, such as Bayer, Dr. Ter Meer is reported to have replied that "no harm had been done to these KZ (concentration camp) inmates as they would have been killed anyway."[28]

My point in stressing Dr. Ter Meer's American corporate connections is not to suggest that corporate executives are possessed of some distinctive quality of villainy. It is to emphasize the extent to which the same attitude of impersonal rationality is required to run successfully a large corporation, a death camp slave labor factory and an extermination center. All three are part of the same world. At least in Germany, the top executives of all three enterprises often felt at home with each other.

Thus, we should not be surprised to learn that social relations were excellent between the resident corporate executives of I. G. Farben's Auschwitz plant and the SS Auschwitz elite. Rudolf Höss, the commandant at Auschwitz, often invited Dr. and Frau Walter Dürrfeld, the head of I. G. Auschwitz, and Dr. and Frau Kurt Eisfeld, the director of I. G. Auschwitz's synthetic rubber division, to his home. While these friendly gatherings were taking place, as many as ten thousand men, women, and children were being exterminated daily.

About 35,000 slaves were used at I. G. Auschwitz. Over 25,000 died. The life expectancy of the average slave in the factory was estimated at between three and four months. Coal was a necessary ingredient in the manufacture of Buna. In the nearby coal mines of I. G. Auschwitz, the life expectancy of the average slave was about one month.[29] Only one incentive was necessary to keep the slaves working at maximum capacity, terror. The workers knew that the moment they were no longer capable of meeting work schedules, they would be sent to the gas chambers. No other incentive was required. None was given. If the slaves did not keep up with the schedule, they were gassed; if they did keep up with it, the work itself killed them within a few months. Their only hope of remaining alive was to maintain a schedule that was calculated finally to kill them. As Weber could not have foreseen the ultimate potentialities of systematic domination given twentieth century technology, neither could Marx or Engels have foreseen the extent to which terror could replace all other incentives in human exploitation. One wonders what refinements might have been added, had the SS possessed computers.

We cannot take leave of I. G. Farben without considering the profit and investment aspect of its involvement at Auschwitz. I. G. Farben was a huge conglomerate. We have noted that its investment in I. G. Auschwitz reached RM 700,000,000. Such an investment could only have been justified by the expectation of a proper return to I. G. Farben's shareholders. Nor were I. G. Farben's profits at Auschwitz limited to its return from the synthetic rubber plant. I. G. Farben also derived handsome profits from the manufacture by its subsidiaries of Zyklon B, the gas used in Auschwitz's chambers.

Zyklon B was the commercial name for a gas used to exterminate rodents and vermin. It had been developed by the *Deutsche Gesellschaft für Schädlingsbekämpfung mbH*, hereafter referred to as DEGESH (German Vermin Combatting Corporation). The shares of DEGESH were held by I. G. Farben (42.5 percent), Deutsche Gold-und Silber-Scheideanstalt (42.5 percent), and Goldschmidt (15 percent). The chairman of DEGESH's administrative committee *(Verwaltungsausschuss)* was an I. G. Farben executive, Generalkonsul Wilhelm R. Mann.

Like many corporations, DEGESH used subcontractors. The actual gas was produced by the *Dessauer Werke für Zucker und Chemische Industrie* and *Kali Werke* A. G. The stabilizer for the gas was produced by I. G. Farben, Uerdinglen. Thus I. G. Farben was both one of DEGESH's co-owners and a subcontractor in the production process. DEGESH did not sell gas directly even to the German government. It controlled two subsidiaries, Heerdt und Lingler GmbH (HELI) and Tesch und Stabenow, *Internationale Gesellschaft für Schadlingsbekämfung mbH* (TESTA). After 1942 Dr. Bruno Tesch became TESTA's sole owner. Sales were divided so that HELI sold primarily to private customers in Germany and TESTA handled the business of the government including Auschwitz.[30]

Hilberg cities one macabre incident that reflected both the moral priorities and the corporate mentality at DEGESH. In March 1944 the Dessau plant was damaged in an air raid. At the time Auschwitz was the only remaining murder center in operation, and the SS was trying to finish off 750,000 Hungarian Jews before it was too late. Because of the bombing, it was impossible to produce Zyklon B with its characteristic odor. The SS was less concerned with the odor than with the effect of the gas. One of its officials requested that five tons of Zyklon B be delivered without the odor-producing element. This troubled a DEGESH official who expressed concern that, without the telltale odor, the company might somehow be in danger of losing its monopoly![31] There was no concern that the gas was being used to kill millions of men and women; there was concern that the company's monopoly in the production of the lethal substance might be compromised.

Both genocide and slave labor proved to be highly profitable corporate enterprises. DEGESH was not a large company. It had a staff of about fifty. Because it was a monopoly, it could and did fix prices. On a relatively meager initial investment of RM 42,500, I. G. Farben received a dividend of RM 85,000 in both 1940 and 1941. In 1942 and 1943 its profits declined from 200 to 100 percent per annum.[32]

To repeat, the business of mass murder was both a highly complex and successful corporate venture. The men who carried out the business part of the venture were not uniformed thugs or hoodlums. They were highly competent, respectable corporate executives who were only doing what they had been trained to do—run large corporations successfully. As long as their institutions functioned efficiently, they had no qualms whatsoever concerning the uses to which they were put.

It is also interesting to note what became of the executives. When the war was over, Theo Goldschmidt of DEGESH became a leading executive of Bayer A. G. of Leverkusen. This was a natural move. Although I. G. Farben was dissolved, its component units continued to function. Goldschmidt simply went from one I. G. Farben subsidiary to another. Hermann Schmitz, the nominal head of I. G. Farben, was sentenced to four years in prison by a U.S. military tribunal. By the mid-fifties he was chairman of the board *(Aufsichrat)* of Rheinische Stahlwerke A. G. Dr. Fritz Ter Meer, the head of Division 2 of I. G. Farben (chemicals, dyes, light metals, and pharmaceuticals) under which I. G. Auschwitz was set up, was sentenced to seven years in prison by a U.S. military tribunal but was released in 1950. He became deputy chairman of T. G. Goldschmidt A. G., Essen, and a member of the boards of the Bankverein Westdeutschland A. G., Düsseldorf and Düsseldorfer Waggonfabrik. Dr. Walter Dürrfeld, the Director of I. G. Auschwitz, received an eight-year sentence but by the mid-fifties he was a director of Scholven-Chemie A. G., Gelsenkirchen. Only Dr. Bruno Tesch, the owner of TESTA, was sentenced to death by a British military court and executed.[33]

Thousands participated in the society of total domination and the murder process. The vast majority of of those *directly* involved were never punished. Most of those still alive hold positions of responsibility and influence in both Germanies. My point in raising this issue is neither to express my own nor to arouse my readers' moral indignation. It is difficult to study the period without becoming convinced of the utter irrelevance of moral indignation as a response to what took place. I am, however, interested in how a society rewards an action taken in its behalf. Verbal expressions of disapproval are cheap. Concrete rewards or punishments provide a better index of how actions are evaluated. These men did "solve" Germany's Jewish problem. This fact was clearly understood by German society which rewarded them and found places of responsibility for them after the war.

Every so often some SS guard who was a participant in one of the mobile killing units that cold-bloodedly shot to death tens of thousands of Jews or who performed some particularly vile task in one of the camps is identified in West Germany and brought to trial. Usually, these people go free "on humanitarian grounds." A few may receive token sentences, such as three or four years for killing ten thousand people, with time off for the period already spent in jail before sentencing. However, as we have seen, almost all of those involved in the corporate enterprises at Auschwitz were were speedily restored to places of leadership in the West German business elite. The tendency towards greater leniency for the business executives reflects an almost universal bias in advanced technological societies. "White-collar crimes," such as large scale embezzlement and corporate fraud, may result in the actual loss of far greater sums of money than the average bank robber or petty thief, yet the "white-collar criminal" is almost always the recipient of greater leniency in the courts.

If there were in reality any *credible* moral standard binding on all human beings and guaranteeing the so-called human rights about which so much has been written, it would be possible to inquire whether the SS guards who received heavier sentences, as they sometimes did, were not unfairly treated in comparison with the business executives. Is there not the suspicion that it is easier to sentence an SS guard than a corporate manager, although the "clean" violence of the latter did the greater damage? A society whose prosperity depends upon virtuosi capable of applying calculating rationality to large-scale corporate enterprise can ill afford the loss of highly trained managerial personnel. It is always easier to find replacements for the lower echelons of the police cadres. When the Russian Revolution broke out, the bourgeoisie and their allies, the officers of the tsarist army, the technicians and the business managers, found themselves suddenly deprived of both wealth and status because they were regarded as "class enemies" of the new regime. Some of the "class enemies" were liquidated in the ensuing violence.

Yet, one of the most important reasons for the ultimate victory of the Red Army over the various counterrevolutionary armies was Leon Trotsky's deliberate decision to recruit former tsarist officers for positions of leadership in the Red Army.[34] Similarly, it was only after the managers, technicians, and specialists were brought back to run the railroads, financial institutions, and factories that Soviet Russia was able to begin to recover from the effects of defeat in World War I, civil war, and foreign intervention. In every modern society those who manage the financial and industrial institutions are a privileged and indispensable elite.

When theologians and students of ethics discuss the question of the validity of some credible set of theonomous or autonomous moral norms governing the conduct of men and nations, they seldom take seriously the well-publicized fact that it was possible for respectable business executives to participate in and profit from a society of total domination and a venture involving the murder of millions of defenseless human beings without losing their elite status in one of the most advanced modern societies. Corporate managers are the kind of men whom society rewards with the greatest financial compensation. They have the easiest access to other elites in government, law, military affairs, and religion. What they are permitted to do—more precisely, what they are rewarded for doing—is a realistic index of what a society regards as within the boundaries of acceptable behavior. By that standard, postwar German society regarded the behavior of the I. G. Farben executives as within the limits of acceptable behavior, at least in wartime. Nor is there any evidence that they were treated leniently because of the peculiar viciousness of German culture. On the contrary, the first steps towards the restoration of their status were usually taken by the special Advisory Board on Clemency set up by the American government to review all sentences on behalf of the American high commissioner for Germany, John J. McCloy, for many years Chairman of the Board of the Chase-Manhattan Bank and a leading establishment figure in the United States.

As the cold war intensified, the sentences meted out in the war crimes trials tended to get ever less severe. Furthermore, few of those convicted were compelled to serve out their terms. Even Oswald Pohl, who was the director of the SS's slave labor program and four leaders of the *Einsatzgruppen*, the mobile killing units, Otto Ohlendorf, Paul Blobel, Werner Braune, and Erich Naumann were regarded almost as martyrs throughout West Germany when all appeals to stay their sentences failed and they were executed by the U.S. Army on June 7, 1951. West German officials argued that it would be less difficult for their country to rearm and join the Western alliance if clemency were shown to those sentenced to prison terms, especially German generals accused of war crimes. American officials felt the pressure and responded accordingly.[35]

Apparently, the Americans did not seriously consider that the West Germans were tied to the United States whether clemency was shown or not. Were it not for the United States, West Germany, and indeed all of Europe, would have fallen under the control of the Soviet Union, as had East Germany and the East European satellites. Most East Germans found Soviet domination far less palatable than cooperation with the United States, as we know from the constant flow of refugees to the west until the erection of the Berlin Wall and the institution of rigid border controls by the D.D.R., the East German government, in August 1961.

Thus, the Germans were not alone in their judgment that the events were not of sufficient weight to warrant more than token punishment. There was apparently an unspoken consensus that the best thing to do with the perpetrators, especially the corporate executives, was to permit them to regain their places in German life.

This does not mean that the majority of those Germans who pleaded for clemency on behalf of those imprisoned for war crimes would have advocated further adventures in the politics of extermination and total domination. Too much had changed as a result of the war. If there was a threat of total domination, its postwar source was the Soviet Union not Germany. There were, in fact, good reasons from the German point of view for urging clemency for almost everybody involved. After 1945 Germany was a society desperately in need of a new beginning. Nothing was less needed than a permanently embittered cadre of ex-Nazis who had no hope of participating in the new society. The Germans understood more clearly than anyone else how difficult it was to draw the line. Once the bureaucratic mechanism of extermination was set in motion, every German was to some extent an active participant, an accomplice or at the very least a beneficiary of the exercise.

Until ethical theorists and theologians are prepared to face without sentimentality the kind of action it is possible freely to perpetrate under conditions of utter respectability in an advanced, contemporary society, none of their assertions about the existence of moral norms will have much credibility. To repeat, no laws were broken and no crimes were committed at Auschwitz. Those who were condemned to the society of total domination were stripped of all protection of the law before they entered. Finally, no credible punishment was meted out. Truly, the twentieth century has been the century par excellence that is beyond good and evil.

As time passes, it becomes apparent that the horrors perpetrated by the Nazis in their society of total domination, such as mutilating and homicidal medical experiments on human beings and corporate utilization of death-camp slave labor, merely carried to a logical conclusion operational attitudes and procedures that are everywhere predominant in the workings of bureaucracy and modern corporate enterprise.*

*This book was written before the LSD experiments on unsuspecting subjects by the Air Force, the Army and the CIA became known.

CHAPTER 5

The Victims' Response:
Bureaucratic Self-Destruction

We have up to this point concentrated on the role of the Germans in creating the extermination project and the society of total domination. However the Germans could not have established such a society by themselves. There had to be compliance on the part of the victims. It is to this subject that we now turn.

The question of Jewish response to the Germans is one of the most painful that arises out of the Holocaust. Any attempt to deal with it is bound to create extraordinary difficulties. Those who have sorrowfully concluded that there was Jewish cooperation in their own undoing, no matter how involuntary, are often accused of desecrating the memory of the dead or even excusing their murderers. The question is especially painful for a Jewish researcher since almost every Jewish family suffered the loss of relatives if not parents or grandparents in the German assault. Within the Jewish community, there has been an understandable tendency to regard those who perished as martyrs whose sanctified memories must not be soiled by the cold-blooded objectivity of political reflection.

Regrettably, those who avoid objective reflection on the Jewish response add to the confusion concerning what took place. Every assault requires at least two actors. Even the most innocent victim is part of the process of his own undoing by virtue of the fact that he did not or could not take protective measures. The very helplessness or ignorance of the victim is an indispensable part of what takes place.

In reality, we know that the leaders of one of Europe's most numerous Jewish communities, the Hungarian, had accurate knowledge of what was taking place, yet they were as little capable of resistance as any of the other Jewish communities. From 1942 to 1944, while most of Europe's Jews were being killed, the Hungarian government, one of Germany's wartime allies, resisted German attempts to take charge of Jews who were Hungarian citizens. The Hungarian government was willing to hand over to the Germans Jews settled in non-Hungarian regions under its control. It was not willing to permit the extermination of its own citizens, although it did subject them to harsh, anti-Semitic measures.

The situation of Hungary's Jews changed radically when the Germans occupied Hungary in March 1944 and began making their own arrangements for the "deportation" of the Jews. According to Dr. Rudolf Kastner, a controversial wartime leader of Hungary's Zionist organization:

In Budapest we had a unique opportunity to follow the fate of European Jewry. We had seen how they had been disappearing one after the other from the map of Europe. At the moment of the occupation of Hungary, the number of dead Jews amounted to over five million. . . . We knew more than was necessary about Auschwitz. . . . We had, as early as 1942, a complete picture of what had happened in the East with the Jews deported to Auschwitz and the other concentration camps.[1]

Yet, in spite of what was known, Adolf Eichmann was able to convince the community's leaders in a single session that they had nothing to fear as long as they cooperated fully with the SS. The cooperation involved Jewish supervision of enforced ghettoization, confiscation of real and personal property, and finally deportation for "labor service" in Poland.[2] Although these were the same measures used by the Germans everywhere to insure the smooth functioning of the extermination program, Hungarian Jews permitted themselves to accept Eichmann's word that *this time* the process would stop short of the final step. Apparently, the horror that awaited them was so great that they chose to grasp at the most pathetic delusion rather than face it. That the delusion was self-imposed can be seen in one of the most extraordinary letters ever written by leaders of a community in modern times. On May 3, 1944, at the height of the savage deportation process, the Central Jewish Council of Hungary wrote a letter seeking an audience with Andor Jarosz, the puppet minister of the interior who had been hand-picked by the Germans to facilitate the deportation of almost 1,000,000 Jews: "We emphatically declare that *we do not seek the audience to lodge complaints about the merit of the measures adopted,* but merely to ask that they be carried out in a humane spirit."[3] (Italics added.) There was to be no protest about mass extermination, only discussion of how to make the deaths easier for the victims. It was actually easier for the Germans to exterminate the Hungarian Jews than it had been for them to kill those who had previously been exterminated. The Hungarian Jewish response is significant because it demonstrates that it made no difference whether a Jewish community knew of the fate that awaited them or not.

One of the elements conditioning the compliant Jewish response to the process of extermination was their own history. The last time the Jews had taken up arms against an enemy was during the Judeo-Roman Wars of 66–70 C.E. and 131–35 C.E. On both occasions, they fought valiantly and lost disastrously. Those who during the first Judaeo-Roman war had counseled submission and surrender were installed by the victors as the religious and political leaders of the Jewish people. The religious leaders of the European diaspora for almost two thousand years were the spiritual heirs of the Pharisees and rabbis who rose to political and religious dominance only after they had been selected by the Romans as their "loyal and nonseditious agents."[4] Thus, diaspora Judaism began in the aftermath of a catastrophic military defeat and survived by developing a culture of surrender and submission in consequence of that defeat. Until the bloody wars with the Romans, the Jews had been a violent, troublesome, rebellious nation. Their transformation from a warrior people of the sword into a submissive people of the book led by plebian scribes and scholars took several generations. By the year 200 C.E., Jewish character had undergone one of the most radical psychological and cultural transformations in history. Rabbinic Judaism is the result of that transformation. It shaped Jewish character and conditioned Jewish responses in the diaspora for two thousand years. Long after Western Jews were secularized and considered themselves "emancipated" from their ancient traditions, they continued as an organized community to respond to overlords as had those who surrendered to the Romans. No matter how grave the provocation, the Jewish community instinctively avoided violent response. They sought to avert hostile action by bribery, petitions for mercy, or appeals to the religious or moral sentiments of their adversaries.

Another Jewish reaction was flight, but, as Hilberg notes, "the Jewish tendency has not been to run from, but to survive with, anti-Jewish regimes."[5] It was the Jewish experience that periods of intensified hostility were often followed by periods of relative mitigation. When all else failed, Jews usually complied with anti-Jewish measures, even if compliance involved submission to rapine and massacre. There was a certain logic to compliance. Even if an adversary wanted to massacre an entire community, there was greater hope that a remnant would survive were the community to abjure resistance. At no time in the two-thousand-year history of diaspora Judaism before the Holocaust were Jews prepared to resist unto death, although they often chose death rather than betray their faith. The ancient example of the defenders of the fortress at Masada, who fought as long as they could and then perished at their own hands rather than surrender to the Romans, was a dim memory that was never reenacted.

During the Holocaust, there was some sporadic resistance to the

Germans, the most spectacular instance of resistance being the 1943 Warsaw Ghetto uprising. Nevertheless, the overwhelming majority of Jews did not resist. They had been conditioned by their religious culture to submit and endure. There was no resort to even token violence when the Nazis forced Jews to dig mass graves, strip, climb into the graves, lie down over the layer of corpses already murdered and await the final coup de grâce. Such submission was the last chapter in the history of a cultural and psychological transformation begun by the rabbis and Pharisees almost two thousand years before.

In addition to the cultural conditioning that affected even the most assimilated Jews, the organized Jewish community was a major factor in preventing effective resistance. Wherever the extermination process was put into effect, the Germans utilized the *existing leadership and organizations* of the Jewish community to assist them. It was not necessary to find traitors or collaborators to do their work. The compliance reaction was automatic. It was only necessary to delegate to the existing Jewish communal leaders the responsibility for transmitting and executing German orders.

The process of taking over the Jewish communal bureaucracies and transforming them into components in the extermination process was one of the organizational triumphs of the Nazis. In the face of the German determination to murder all Jews, most Jews instinctively relied on their own communal organizations to defend their interests whenever possible. Unfortunately, these very organizations were transformed into subsidiaries of the German police and state bureaucracies.

This process can be seen best in the transformation of the *Reichsvertretung der Juden in Deutschland* (Reich Representation of Jews in Germany) into the *Reichsereinigung der Juden in Deutschland* (Reich Association of Jews in Germany). The *Reichsvertretung* was established in 1933 by the Jewish community as its official agency to enter into dialogue with the new regime concerning the future of Jews in Germany.[6] In 1939 by Nazi decree it became the *Reichsvereinigung*. Its purpose was to serve as the officially designated Jewish agency responsible for transmitting and executing all German measures concerning the

Jews within the Reich. The *Reichsvertretung* had been established by Jews to represent their interests. They chose the most distinguished German Jewish rabbi of the twentieth century, Leo Baeck, as their leader. When the Nazis took over Rabbi Baeck continued as leader. He was fully convinced that his tragic role would mitigate the hazards facing his people.

At first, the *Reichsvereinigung* performed the bureaucratic preliminary work necessary for the later stages of the destruction process. Jewish statisticians informed the SS of births, deaths, and other demographic changes. The communal newspaper *(Jüdisches Nachrichtenblatt)* kept people informed of German decrees. Jewish bureaucrats sat at their desks and performed the tasks assigned to them by German bureaucrats further up the chain of authority. According to Weber, "The principles of office hierarchy and of levels of graded authority mean a firmly ordered system of super- and subordination in which there is a supervision of the lower offices by the higher ones."[7] One of the most important reasons for the system of graded authority in a bureaucracy, according to Weber, is that the subordinate must fulfill assigned tasks "without any will of his own." As subordinates, the Jewish bureaucrats had no effective will of their own.

The transformation of the bureaucracy of the Jewish community into a functioning component of the Nazi bureaucracy reached a point of no return in 1941 when both the Gestapo and the Jewish communal agencies responsible for facilitating Jewish emigration from Germany were charged with a new responsibility, that of drawing up lists of Jews for "deportation" and "resettlement" in the East. Neither the personnel nor the names of the agencies were changed. Both the Gestapo and the Jewish bureaucrats were still engaged in the task of facilitating Jewish emigration, but emigration now took on a new and sinister meaning. When, for example, Adolf Eichmann appeared on the scene in Vienna immediately after the German entry into the city in 1938, he used every means at his disposal to encourage voluntary emigration from the Reich. After the "final solution" became official policy, he was, according to his own account, still involved in emigration and "transport" work.[8] The difference was that "emigration" was now involuntary and the destination of the émigrés was the death camps.

Thus, the official agency of German Jews led by the most distinguished German rabbi of the twentieth century, a man in whose memory an important rabbinical seminary has been named (London's Leo Baeck College), undertook such tasks as selecting those who were to be deported, notifying the families and, finally, of sending the Jewish police to round up the victims. In the Warsaw Ghetto and in Lodz, Poland, the Jewish council, or *Judenrat*, did not resist German directives even when the Germans demanded the "selection" of 10,000 Jews a day for deportation. Jewish bureaucrats made the selection; Jewish police rounded up the victims.[9]

Undoubtedly, Rabbi Baeck and most of those who led the *Judenräte*, the Nazi-dominated Jewish councils in the occupied territories, were convinced that somehow a remnant would survive if German orders were strictly obeyed. In the past, there had always been a remnant. In the case of Baeck, his commitment to lawfulness was so complete that when the Gestapo finally came to deport him to the "privileged" concentration camp at Theresienstadt in Czechoslovakia, he asked for a little time to arrange his affairs. Before leaving on his journey to the camp, he mailed postal money orders covering his gas and electric bills![10]

The subject of the *Judenräte* has been explored by Isaiah Trunk and other scholars.[11] It is impossible for any one who did not experience their tragic fate to stand in judgment. Our purpose is to understand a process, not to judge its victims. It is, however, undeniable that Jewish communal organizations everywhere were transformed into functioning components of the German bureaucratic mechanism devoted to the "final solution." As such, they facilitated the process in at least two crucial ways: (a) In almost all of the killing operations, the German personnel were short-handed. It is estimated that only fifty SS personnel and 200 Lett and Ukrainian auxiliaries were assigned to the Warsaw Ghetto which had a population of five hundred thousand at its peak, almost all of whom perished.[12] Every task performed by the *Judenräte* lessened the drain on German resources. (b) The only organization to which Jews could turn and which might have provided a political base for resistance was in fact a component of the German machinery of death.

Under any circumstance, the Jews were doomed. German power was overwhelming and there was in fact no hope of assistance from any other quarter. Given the choice of accepting the German offer of a "mercy death" or of attempting unarmed, individual resistance, it was undoubtedly wiser to dig one's own grave, lie down in it and await the final blow. The Germans were capable of inflicting infinitely worse deaths. Resistance is only consequential when it is *organized*. In the face of inevitable doom, a resistance movement must at least provide a means of preventing its members from falling into the hands of the enemy. When the defenders of Masada concluded that they were doomed, they were able to deny the Roman adversary the opportunity of torturing them to death. Their deaths were their own. Hence, they were able to inflict maximum damage on the enemy before taking their leave. Only an *organized* group has hope of inflicting serious damage on an overwhelmingly powerful enemy.

When the doomed remnant of the Warsaw Ghetto finally decided to organize and fight the Germans, its first task was to create a noncollaborating organization that could destroy the *Judenrat*'s authority over the Jewish community. Before taking action against the Germans, the resistance movement first killed the chief of the Jewish police, Joseph Szerynski, a Jew converted to Catholicism. They also killed his successor and struck at other Jewish police and known collaborators. Only after they had violently displaced the *Judenrat* could they move against the Germans.[13]

The Warsaw resistance was atypical. Almost everywhere else, the *Judenräte* maintained their authority until the leaders of the *Judenräte*, their usefulness to the Germans at an end, were themselves sent to their deaths.

In most of the countries occupied by the Nazis during the war and by the invading Soviet armies after the war, the state bureaucracies were taken over by the invaders and turned into components of the invader's structure of domination. Some elements of each state or police bureaucracy were, of course, regarded as "unreliable" or as "objective enemies" of the new order. Nevertheless, most members of the bureaucracy continued to function efficiently and obediently *"sine ira et studio,"* without scorn or bias, for their new masters. There was, of course, an enormous difference between the aims of the Soviet occupation of Eastern Europe and the earlier occupation by the Nazis. The Soviets were interested in dominating the states on their border and preventing a reunion of the two Germanies on terms unfavorable to their security requirements. Soviet domination of Eastern Europe was closer to that of a classical tyranny than was the German occupation. The German aims were far more radical. They sought to create a society of total domination involving initially the enslavement and extermination of the Jews and eventually similar treatment to other subject peoples. They were determined to clear a *Lebensraum,* a living space, for German settlement. This could only be done by the expulsion, enslavement, and extermination of the conquered territory's former occupants. German occupation thus revealed the full potentialities of bureaucratically organized, systematic domination far more completely than that of the Soviet Union. *The Germans demonstrated that a modern state can successfully organize an entire people for its own extermination.* They have also demonstrated that there are forces at work in modern society, in both aggressors and victims, that were completely beyond the comprehension of the liberal, enlightened imagination until it was forced to face their actuality. It may be argued that the Jews were a special case, that they were rendered incapable of anything but compliance both by their peculiar history and by the nearly universal consent with which their undoing was met. Against such an argument, there is the fact that, with no less ease, the Germans were also able to exterminate a large number of Gypsies, Poles, and Russian prisoners of war. In his essay on bureaucracy, Max Weber observed that

the apparatus, with its peculiar impersonal character . . . is easily made to work for anybody who knows how to gain control over it. A rationally ordered system of officials continues to function smoothly after the enemy has occupied the area: he merely needs to change the top officials. [14]

With the Jewish community, it was not even necessary to change the top officials, even when they were revered and distinguished rabbis. Here as elsewhere, Weber's observations are prophetic, although it is doubtful that he could have realized the extremities to which they could apply. If nothing else, the fact that the best and most selfless Jewish leaders presented no greater obstacle when the Nazis took over their communities than did the most opportunistic raises some very terrifying questions about the potentialities of bureaucratic domination in modern society. And, as we have noted, the Nazis didn't even have computers.

CHAPTER 6

Reflections on
A Century of Progress*

There is much more that could be written about the Holocaust. It should, however, be clear that the Holocaust was something very different than an outburst of monumental violence and hatred such as the massacres that have all too frequently punctuated human history. Recently, such incidents as the massacre at My-Lai and the Palestinian terrorist attack on Israeli school children at Maalot have been likened to genocide on a small scale. The Holocaust was qualitatively different from both. The terrorists at Maalot were capable of indiscriminate killing; they were neither capable of nor interested in organizing their victims into a society of total domination, as were the SS.

Similarly, there is no way that the alleged actions of Lieutenant William Calley and his associates, as deplorable as they were, can be

---

*This was the optimistic title given to the Chicago World's Fair which opened its doors in the midst of the Great Depression in 1933, the year of Hitler's assumption of power. The theme of the fair was expressed in the slogan: "Science Explores: Technology Executes: Mankind Conforms." Cf. Lewis Mumford, *The Myth of the Machine* (New York: Harcourt Brace Jovanovitch, 1970) p. 213.

likened to Auschwitz. From all accounts about My-Lai, it would appear that the massacre took place because the Americans *lost control* of themselves under conditions of wartime stress. Auschwitz was made possible because the German bureaucracy and the SS were *in control* at every step.

At Auschwitz, the Germans revealed new potentialities in the human ability to dominate, enslave, and exterminate. They also revealed new areas in which capitalist enterprise might profitably and even respectably be employed. The camps were thus far more of a permanent threat to the human future than they would have been had they functioned solely as an exercise in mass killing. An execution center can only manufacture corpses; a society of total domination creates a world of the living dead that can serve as a prototype of a future social order, especially in a world confronted by catastrophic crises and ever-increasing, massive population redundancy.

As we know, the twentieth century has witnessed extraordinary "progress" in the unlimited intensification of human destructiveness and the radicalization of the forms of human domination. *Nevertheless, it was the organizational skill of the Nazis rather than their new weapons that made the society of total domination a reality.* And, most of the organizational tools with which such a society can be set up have been greatly improved since World War II. Of supreme importance as a weapon of bureaucratic domination is the modern computer. Few weapons were as indispensable to the Gestapo as its files. When one compares the laborious task of maintaining comprehensive files as short a time back as World War II with the instantaneous retrieval of data about anyone the police or any other governmental agency might be interested in today, we see how greatly the problem of keeping tabs on people has been simplified.

Once a system of domination has been demonstrated to be a capability of government, it invites repetition. There are a number of circumstances in which a future ruler of a modern state might be tempted to install his own version of such a system. At the crudest level, government by bureaucratically organized, rationalized terror simplifies the problem of command, especially in a bitterly divided society. Those classes or groups who for economic, racial, religious, or social reasons oppose the program of the dominant elite could find themselves condemned to detention camps or eliminated altogether. The liquidation of the peasants under Stalin is a good example of the use of such terror. When the Bolsheviks seized power in 1917, Lenin promised the peasants that they would gain land from the dispossessed aristocracy and the government. In reality, Lenin was committed by ideology to the abolition of private agricultural holdings and the rationalization of farming as a large-scale collective enterprise.[1] When the peasants realized that it was their destiny under Bolshevism to be proletarianized, they naturally resisted. Under Stalin the conflict between the government's determination to rationalize agricultural production and the peasants' unwillingness to be proletarianized was resolved by the extermination of millions of peasants and the terrorization of the rest.[2]

Even in the United States, the scandals associated with the Nixon presidency revealed the early stages of a similar tendency. The Nixon presidency shared several characteristics with the totalitarian rulers of the twentieth century: (a) In the period immediately after his reelection in 1972, when opposition was at its lowest point, Nixon intensified rather than diminished his overt hostility to his opponents both within and outside of government. (b) Nixon had an unfortunate tendency not to distinguish between methods that are appropriate in dealing with domestic political opponents and foreign adversaries. One of the gravest threats to constitutional government posed by foreign ventures is the possibility that government leaders might ignore constitutional restraints and employ the kind of "dirty" tactics they customarily use against foreigners in dealing with domestic opposition. That is why any domestic use of the CIA is so great a threat to American freedom. The domestic spying activities and the raid on the office of Dr. Lewis Fielding, Daniel Ellsberg's psychiatrist, by members of the extralegal White House "plumbers" unit are examples of the use of CIA trained personnel and the CIA itself, in domestic political conflicts. And, it is hardly likely that we will ever know the whole story of those episodes. (c) Nixon sought to secure consent to his program, if not by physical terror, then certainly by the beginnings of bureaucratic terror. Perhaps this was best seen in his attempts to utilize the Internal Revenue Service to harass political opponents as well as public personalities whose style of life or political commitments were distasteful to him. In addition to tax harassment, there were other attempts at bureaucratic harassment such as the threat to revoke the licenses of television stations owned by the Washington Post. The intent of the threatened punitive action was clear: opponents were warned that there were heavy penalties involved in opposing Richard Nixon. Such use of power was an important initial step in the direction of government by terror. Fortunately, the administrators of the most important government agency involved, the Internal Revenue Service, were seldom willing to go along.[3] In this respect the federal bureaucracy, whatever its faults, still retained a measure of independence from the chief executive, something the German bureaucracy felt honor bound *not to do* after Hitler's accession to power.

It may seem a long way from the improper use of the Internal Revenue Service, the FBI, the CIA and other federal agencies to harass opponents to a society of total domination, but Nixon had taken several important steps in that direction. He attempted to replace the give and take of the normal American political process by bureaucratic harassment. Fear was to replace debate and persuasion. In addition, he had established a category of citizens, the so-called "enemies' lists," who were to be subject to punitive government action, although they had broken no law and for whom there was no legal justification for any kind of government hostility. Those who had opposed him had, in fact, done nothing more than exercise their normal right to take a stand on political issues.

We must remember that the German concentration camps were originally set up to detain and punish those who had broken no law and against whom no punitive action could legally be justified. Nixon and his staff did not propose anything as radical as permanent detention camps, but they did seek extralegal methods of punishing political adversaries.

Among the bitter lessons of the Nixon administration is that an American president can be tempted to resort, if not to overt terror, at least to extralegal bureaucratic harassment to secure the compliance of the governed. And, if the Nazi period has any political moral, it is that bureaucratically planned and executed domination can be more thorough-going and effective than all other systems of domination. Furthermore, the discovery of the Watergate break-in was a fortunate accident. At the beginning of the second term, the Nixon administration had openly demonstrated its contempt for the legislative branch and its intention to deprive the federal bureaucracy of any residual independence. It is not pleasant to contemplate the measures the Nixon administration might have taken had it been able to proceed without hindrance. Because of Watergate, Nixon's ability to employ extralegal means of harassment was unexpectedly curtailed. Were it not for Watergate, the Nixon presidency might have proceeded from relatively mild to ever more radical measures. At each step along the way, Nixon's ability to silence opposition would probably have fallen short of expectations. The tax and licensing harassment would not have created the fear they were intended to. It is difficult to believe that, once embarked on an extralegal course, the Nixon administration would have accepted failure without attempting ever more radical measures.

It would be comforting to think that the abuses of power that occurred in the Nixon administration were due solely to his moral and political shortcomings. Unfortunately, the problem will not go away with the departure of Richard Nixon. The abuses occurred because *the structure of government* put the capacity to act as did Nixon in the hands of any president willing to employ it and clever enough to get away with such behavior. The bureaucracy that Nixon sought to use extralegally might be so used by a future president. Should, for example, the economic crisis continue to deteriorate or should a catastrophic war break out, a future president might be tempted by the readiness of a desperate nation to accept radical measures in order to solve its woes. The overwhelming power of modern government is bound to increase no matter who is president. And not every President will be as clumsy or as noncharismatic as Nixon.

Nixon was tempted to expand the power available to him because of his inability to effectuate his program through the normal political processes. There are other reasons why a future political leader might be tempted to utilize the full power of government available to him. The population problem figures strongly in all such calculations. The Nazi extermination program is, unfortunately, of great relevance in any discussion of the problem of population. In terms of German ideology, the Jews were a *surplus population* because of the kind of society the Germans wanted to create. In the foreseeable future, there will be forces other than ideology that will create mammoth surplus populations throughout the world. For the time being the balance between surplus population and limited resources is being restored by the most natural of means—famine. In the future, famine may no longer be a politically acceptable method of restoring the balance between population and resources, especially were such crises to arise in the more developed countries. A Nazi-type "solution" might appear more acceptable politically to some social planners than the haphazard elimination occasioned by famine. Extermination would have the advantage of allowing a government to choose the categories of people it will sacrifice. A country with limited capital resources and excess population might attempt to rationalize its agricultural and industrial productivity by a combination of slave labor and eventual mass extermination of those reduced to slavery. Such a use of slavery could accelerate agricultural and industrial growth and eliminate the population excess at the same time. Whatever the future may bring, it is certain that the pressure of population on resources will continue to grow. In the eyes of some future social planners, the Nazi extermination program might appear to be an efficient and rational solution to the problem. It is my intention to discuss this issue in detail in the forthcoming, companion volume to this book.

Some may argue that such a scenario has a certain plausibility, but its nightmarish character demonstrates the need to find a way to reduce the number of births through effective planned parenthood. Unfortunately, the scenario of effective birth control indoctrination among the poor lacks plausibility. It has failed in most of the underdeveloped countries. In times of heightened stress, government bureaucrats might feel that they have no choice but to turn to compulsory measures. They might regard those who insist on having more than the officially set quota of children as engaging in "antisocial behavior." One American population expert has already used that designation.[4] Some bureaucrat might study the Nazi plans for mass sterilization such as the proposal to sterilize inmates unwittingly as they stood at a counter filling out forms. Compulsory sterilization or vasectomy might seem like a reasonable "solution." Then too, there is infanticide which was always a population control measure.[5] In ancient times infanticide could be made acceptable by the conviction that the children were being offered up as an acceptable sacrifice to the gods. Both morally and emotionally, it was probably easier to offer children to the gods than to a government-sponsored program of population control.

Future bureaucrats might be tempted to set up extermination centers to keep the size of the population from getting out of hand. However, even with a stable population, there are circumstances under which such centers might prove to be a temptation. It is, for example, argued that only zero population growth can avoid the coming Malthusian catastrophe. But zero population growth might mean the end of the economic advantages inherent in moderate population growth and an intensification of hostility within society through competition for an inelastic number of desirable vocational slots. Because of the declining birth rate and the end of the Vietnam war, the teaching profession has already been adversely affected. In certain academic disciplines with a limited clientele, graduate students and junior faculty keep tabs on the holders of every major chair, waiting for the incumbents to die or retire so that they may have a chance to move up a very small and overcrowded ladder. Encouragement of early retirement is one way in which room can be made for younger personnel. At present, early retirement often condemns talented men and women to a semivegetating existence. The hand of the future may be already visible in what can only be called the inflation-induced pension swindle. Men and women who deferred a portion of their earnings in the hope that they would be available after retirement find that inflation increasingly deprives them of the resources with which to survive. Thus, an implicit promise made by society is not kept. Inflation involves a discount on the promises inherent in paper money as a claim on the goods and services available in an organized society. What we are currently seeing is only the tip of the iceberg. It is conceivable that what lies ahead is a condition involving both zero population growth and a world-wide depletion of resources. In such a circumstance, the old saying that those who do not work will not eat could take on ominous meaning. Bureaucrats in some countries might someday decree compulsory early retirement and, at the same time, grant the retirees "a mercy death." The social advantages are obvious. The most vigorous elements in society would constitute its work force and there would be no claim on society's resources by superannuated or economically redundant elements. Such a program would also represent a continuation of present trends in which the human rather than the natural order increasingly determines our conditions of life and death. Death would finally cease to be a natural and would become almost entirely a political finality. This scenario is by no means farfetched. According to Hannah Arendt, the mammoth Stalinist purges of the thirties performed exactly those functions. A whole new class of officeholders succeeded to the positions of the millions Stalin had eliminated. Furthermore, none of the resources of Russian society had to be allocated either to the detention or the pensioning of those who were purged.[6]

There is a variant of the granting of a "mercy death" to early retirees. In a multiethnic society, the dominant ethnic majority might retain scarce jobs and resources for itself and eliminate competing minorities.[7] That, in effect, is what the Germans did. We know to what extremes men with power can be driven under conditions of stress. Is it possible, for example, that some future American administration might solve the problem of non-white "welfare loafers" who are "too lazy to work" by such measures? Some of the excessively harsh statements made about people on welfare by members of the Nixon administration and their supporters contained a note of resentment and even racial hostility. Those who made such statements did not seem to understand the extent to which the poor were victims of oceanic economic and social movements entirely beyond their control. Today resentment at supporting the poor takes verbal expression. However, such resentment could become draconian should the resources available to sustain the poor disappear. There could come a time when bureaucrats might attempt to eliminate all of the ills associated with urban blight, such as crime, drugs, and unsafe streets, by eliminating those segments of the population that are regarded as most prone to social pathology. The Germans had such a program in mind when they planned to eliminate "asocials" from German society by exterminating them.

My purpose in suggesting these unpleasant scenarios is neither to play the prophet nor to predict the future. The scenarios are admittedly images of extremity, but can anyone be assured after the Nixon presidency that no future president will resort to radical measures in a crisis? Let us not forget that it was Franklin D. Roosevelt who put over one hundred thousand Japanese Americans in concentration camps. My purpose is rather to point out that the explosive combination of surplus population, finite resources, and the expanding sovereign powers of government suggest that the Nazi extermination program may yet foreshadow other exercises in the politics of total domination by future governments as they face catastrophic population problems arising out of mankind's very success in mastering nature.

As we have seen, large-scale destruction is not without its rewards. In the Soviet Union, in spite of the terror engendered by Stalin's purges, those Russians who were promoted to the emptied vocational slots did benefit from the slaughter. Whatever Stalin's personal motives may have been, his policies had the effect of ridding the Soviet Union of a potentially surplus population. It is very likely that Stalin played a role in Russia similar to that of Field Marshall Haig and General von Falkenhayn in World War I. Very similar historical forces may have been operative in all three leaders. If such were indeed the case, we would have to conclude that, at least in mass society, men are not and perhaps cannot be in control of their own destiny, but that their grim, consuming destiny unfolds beyond their intentions and behind their backs.

One of the most difficult conclusions to which we have come in this reflection on Auschwitz is that the Nazis committed no crime at Auschwitz since no law or political order protected those who were first condemned to statelessness and then to the camps. That observation was not offered as a defense of the Nazis. On the contrary, it was offered as an unpleasant example of the ironic and unanticipated consequences of the spread of "civilization" and "progress" so that today no corner of the earth lacks some form of political organization. Unfortunately, the demise of the Third Reich has not put an end to the problem of statelessness. Sooner or later there will be other civil or international conflicts that will deprive large numbers of men of the most elemental of human rights, their membership in a political order, with consequences as yet unforeseen.

Yet, if Auschwitz has taught us the hazards of statelessness, it can also teach us that membership in a political community is no longer a guarantee of the most elemental human rights. With the collapse of every credible religious and moral restraint on the state and with the inevitable depersonalization of the relations between the rulers and the ruled, the state's sovereignty can achieve an ultimacy unimpeded by any contending claim. In the American system, the citizen is still protected by a series of constitutional restraints on the state's power. Nevertheless, we have already seen how the Nixon administration attempted to ignore those restraints and no one can tell what a Nixon-like administration might do in the future. In any event, no one questions the legal right of the state to execute its citizens when they have been given the benefit of due process of the law, but no one has been able to set quantitative limits to the right of execution. Furthermore, the Jews were executed in accordance with German law, and it is not inconceivable that the slaughter of World War I was an unwitting form of mass execution visited by governments on their own men.

The unlimited character of the state's sovereignty even in the extermination of its own citizens was recognized by Justice Robert Jackson, the presiding American judge at the Nuremberg war crimes trials. Jackson expressed the opinion that the Nazis involved in the extermination of the Jews could not be prosecuted for murdering Jews of German nationality. He argued that no state can sit in judgment of another's treatment of its minorities. Jackson felt compelled to assert the ultimacy of national sovereignty over all conflicting claims, even the right to life itself. He did not, of course, approve of the Nazi actions. He sought to include the extermination project in the catalogue of war crimes, but only because the project was pursued as part of a war of unjustified aggression, not because the extermination was a crime in itself.[8] The right of a state to define the conditions under which capital punishment will be inflicted has not been impaired by the Holocaust.

It is sometimes argued that there is a higher moral law against which the deeds of men and nations are measured. The International War Crimes Trials held at Nuremberg after the war were supposed to have been based upon the premise that there were norms by which the Nazis could be held to account. Unfortunately, the outcome of the trials demonstrated that, if such norms exist, there is little or no penalty for their violation. And, norms that can freely be violated are as good as none at all.

As we have noted, the verdicts in the war crimes trials tended to become progressively more lenient as the cold war heated up, thus indicating that extralegal considerations played an important part in what was alleged to have been a judicial process. It can, however, be argued that the extralegal considerations are evidence that the trials had nothing to do with law.[9] There was no common law binding both the Third Reich and the Allies. The SS personnel were faithfully carrying out their duties in accordance with the law of their country.

The Nuremberg trials were not a giant step forward in international law. They were in all likelihood an elaborate exercise in national vengeance. In ancient times it was not considered the function of the state to punish private injury. The greatest deterrent against the would-be aggressor was his calculation of the victim's ability to avenge a wrong, either alone or in concert with members of his family or tribe.[10] The ancient law of tribal vengeance may have been primitive but, in the absence of any impartial public institution for meting out punishment, it did serve to contain violence. The need for the Nuremberg trials arose out of a similar situation: there was no disinterested supranational institution that could enact and enforce laws binding on sovereign states. The situation between sovereign states is not unlike that which in ancient times led to the law of tribal vengeance. The power to injure remains the most credible deterrent to a would-be aggressor's violence. At Nuremberg the Allies avenged wrongs done to themselves and their clients. Those who had the power could avenge. The Jews had no power and the interest of the Allies in acting on their behalf diminished radically as West German military cooperation against the Soviet bloc assumed importance.

By the same logic, the trial of Adolf Eichmann in Jerusalem in 1961 can be seen as a symbolic act of vengeance by the Israeli government that had neither the power nor the interest to hunt down every last participant in the extermination project but wanted to use Eichmann as a surrogate for all those whom it could not punish.[11] Some may claim that vengeance is indefensible in a world of evolving, higher moral sensibilities, yet it is difficult to see what other deterrent can exist in a world in which a legal system is binding within a state but never between political communities.

The dreadful history of Europe's Jews has demonstrated that *rights do not belong to men by nature.* To the extent that men have rights, they have them only as members of the polis, the political community, and there is no polis or Christian commonwealth of nations. All that men possess by nature is the necessity to participate in the incessant life and death struggle for existence of any animal. Furthermore, unlike other animals, men have no fixed instinctual structure that regulates their behavior and limits their aggression against members of the same species. Outside of the polis there are no inborn restraints on the human exercise of destructive power.

When the Nazis sought to justify to themselves the extermination project, they often used arguments from nature.[12] They argued that in nature it is the fate of the weak to perish. The Nazi argument rested upon the accurate perception that no political order upheld the rights of their victims or defined the relations between warring nations. In nature men have the same rights as flies, mosquitoes or beasts of prey. The Nazis emphasized this by using language that indicated that their victims had been expelled from the human world of politics and condemned at best to the status of beasts of burden.

When men and women reflect on the theological significance of Auschwitz, they tend to reduce the issue to the problem of theodicy. How, they ask, could the all-wise, all-powerful Lord of History have permitted so great an evil? Undoubtedly, the question of God and human evil is one of the most serious problems arising out of the Holocaust.[13] However, there are other issues of more immediate consequence. To the best of my knowledge, no theologian has attempted to deal with the problems implicit in the fact that the Nazis probably committed no crime at Auschwitz. The natural temptation of theologians would be to assert the existence of either a natural or a God-ordained law binding upon all men and nations in terms of which the Holocaust can be judged. Unfortunately, even if it were possible to prove that such a law exists, it is difficult to see what practical difference that would make in the arena of contemporary politics.

Let us assume that such a law exists and that leaders of the major religions could agree on its contents. What would be the penalties for violating it and the means whereby it could be enforced? In an earlier age, men and women genuinely stood in awe of the punitive wrath of divinity, but is this any longer true? Does not the Holocaust demonstrate that there are absolutely no limits to the degradation and assault the managers and technicians of violence can inflict upon men and women who lack the power of effective resistance? If there is a law that is devoid of all penalty when violated, does it have any functional significance in terms of human behavior? Is not a law which carries no penalties functionally equivalent to no law at all? Even if it could be demonstrated that it exists, can it not be safely ignored? We are sadly forced to conclude that we live in a world that is *functionally* godless and that human rights and dignity depend upon the power of one's community to grant or withhold them from its members.

Thus, the Holocaust bears witness to *the advance of civilization,* I repeat, to the advance of civilization, to the point at which large scale massacre is no longer a crime and the state's sovereign powers are such that millions can be stripped of their rights and condemned to the world of the living dead. Thus, the process of secularization ends where it began. In the beginning secularization involved the demystification of and the limitation of the sovereign's power. In the end, the secular state has dethroned all mystifications of power and morality save its own. The state becomes the only true god on earth with the power to define realistically what is good and will be rewarded and what is evil and will be punished; this truly sovereign god also has the ultimate power of divinity, the power to decide who shall live and who shall die. No cold-blooded contemporary David need worry about a modern Nathan the prophet proclaiming the ultimacy of God's law. That day is over, never to return, unless some apocalyptic catastrophe destroys Western civilization as we know it and compels mankind to begin again out of the nuclear ruins. This does not mean that the sovereign can not be limited; he can, but only by the laws of men acting in concert, at best a tenuous guarantee of a humane society. Fortunately, the American political system has insisted until now upon limitations on the chief executive's power. And, it is a good thing. Otherwise, there might be no limit to the tyrannies a modern ruler might inflict upon those whom he governs.

Similarly, if it is no crime for a state to exterminate its citizens or subject peoples, it is also no crime to inflict upon them the kind of slavery the Nazis inflicted upon the camp inmates. This fact was as clearly understood by the Bolsheviks as by the Nazis. Both the Nazis and the Bolsheviks under Stalin have demonstrated that a properly organized modern state can inflict total domination upon any segment of its population it chooses. Unfortunately, there are no categories arising out of traditional political, religious, or ethical norms with which such problems can realistically be confronted. It is, of course, possible to reiterate traditional affirmations about the innate dignity of human beings, but the existence of bureaucratically administered societies of total domination is the most compelling empirical refutation of all such claims. In the face of the new forms of domination, assertions about innate human dignity are either false or meaningless.

Nor is it likely that an uncritical attempt to return to the Judeo-Christian tradition will yield a credible reaffirmation of the humanistic values that have been dissolved by the all-conquering rationality of modern political and economic structures. On the contrary, the Judeo-Christian tradition is itself part of the problem. If it is possible to suggest an analogy from psychology, just as depth psychology was able to expose the ineradicable dark side of human personality even in those situations in which men appear most loving and altruistic, so the world of the death camps and the society it engenders reveals the progressively intensifying night side of Judeo-Christian civilization. Civilization means slavery, wars, exploitation, and death camps. It also means medical hygiene, elevated religious ideals, beautiful art, and exquisite music. *It is an error to imagine that civilization and savage cruelty are antitheses. On the contrary, in every organic process, the antitheses always reflect a unified totality, and civilization is an organic process.* Mankind never emerged out of savagery into civilization. Mankind moved from one type of civilization involving its distinctive modes of both sanctity and inhumanity to another. In our times the cruelties, like most other aspects of our world, have become far more effectively administered than ever before. They have not and they will not cease to exist. Both creation and destruction are inseparable aspects of what we call civilization.

Even, nay especially, religion has its night side. Thus, we have offered the hypothesis that the secularization process that led to bureaucracy, capitalism, and the society of total domination was the outcome of the biblical tradition. Without that tradition, or at least the ethos it engendered, it is likely that neither fully rationalized bureaucracy nor the death camps would have developed. Nor can we ignore the biblical roots of the hideous Nazi caricature of the Chosen People doctrine, the claim that pure-blooded Germans are a *Herrenvolk,* a master race, destined to rule, enslave or exterminate non-Germans. It is fashionable to see anticipations of Nazi anti-Semitism in Germany's greatest religious figure, Martin Luther, but it is seldom acknowledged that Luther's intolerance and hatred was thoroughly biblical in its rejection of those who do not maintain whatever is construed to be fidelity to the only true word of the Lord. All this is a part of the night side of religion. What makes the problem so serious is that there is no escape from the self-defeating ethos of exclusivism and intolerance we have described as long as our fundamental culture is derived from a religious tradition that insists upon the dichotomous division of mankind into the elect and the reprobate. And there is only one way in which the Judeo-Christian tradition in its secularized if not its religious forms could be overcome: a mammoth world-wide catastrophe in which hundreds of millions of human beings are destroyed and civilization as we know it disappears among the crazed, frightened survivors. Such a scenario is plausible; we have the weaponry to bring it about. Unfortunately, the traumatic cure of the illness we call Judeo-Christian civilization would prove infinitely worse than the disease itself.

The illness we call Judeo-Christian civilization? Perhaps it is well, before we conclude, to recall some ancient and modern myths about the origins of civilization. The liberal-humanist tradition of faith in the upward march of civilization flies in the face of what some of the greatest mythmakers of the western world have told us about ourselves and our culture. In the Judeo-Christian tradition itself, the human order is depicted as beginning with an act of primal disobedience on the part of the original progenitor of the race. Dwelling effortlessly in Paradise, Adam cannot rest content with a world that requires neither cleverness nor organizational intelligence to yield all that he wishes. What he is and what he possesses in original innocence is not sufficient for him. The consequences of Adam's *Fall* are the beginnings of history and culture.

Whatever its limitations, the Judeo-Christian tradition understood that, far from being an achievement, civilization requires a savior to extricate mankind from its consequences.

Sigmund Freud's myth is equally pessimistic about civilization. The brothers of the original protohuman horde cannot restrain their envy of their tyrannical father and, most especially, his sexual prerogatives. They want his position of dominance and the women that go with it. They murder him to get both. The system of undoing they create to alleviate their feelings of guilt is for Freud the beginning of our morality, religion, and culture. We are all, according to Freud, the heirs of the guilt-ridden fraternity of murderers. In each generation we are tempted to repeat their parricide; in each generation we are afflicted by their guilt. And the ineradicable guilt, far from rendering us contrite, drives us on to ever greater excesses. [14]

Hegel's myth of the origin of civilization, the dialectic of the master and the slave, is a tale of combat and domination. Two self-consciousnesses meet. Each sees the other as a threat. A life and death struggle ensues in which one fears for his life and chooses to submit to the other. He prefers life as a slave to no life whatsoever. The victor becomes the master because of his greater capacity for violence and his indifference to whether he lives or dies. Thus, according to Hegel, arises the first human community in which "we" can be spoken. It is founded upon domination, exploitation, and smoldering resentment. Henceforth, the slave awaits his hour to turn the tables. And the beginning of things, the life and death struggle for dominance, reveals their nature thereafter. [15] All three myths are in accord with our fundamental thesis: Twentieth century bureaucratized violence in all of its manifestations is an expression of contemporary Western civilization rather than a rebellion against it.

Perhaps it was no accident that the most highly urbanized people in the Western world, the Jews, were the first to perish in the ultimate city of Western civilization, Necropolis, the new city of the dead that the Germans built and maintained at Auschwitz. Auschwitz was perhaps the terminal expression of an urban culture that first arose when an ancient protobourgeoisie liberated its work life from the haphazard, unpredictable, and seasonable character of agriculture and sustained itself by work which was, in the words of Max Weber, "continuous and rational." In the beginning, removed from immediate involvement in "the vital realities of nature," the city was the habitat of the potter, the weaver, the carpenter, and the scribe; in the end, it houses the police bureaucrat and his corporate counterpart coldly and methodically presiding over the city of the dead.

There is always the danger that Metropolis will become Necropolis. The city is by nature antinature, antiphysis, and, hence, antilife. The world of the city, *our world*, is the world of human invention and power; it is also the world of artifice, dreams, charades, and the paper promises we call money. But even the richest and most powerful city can only survive as long as the umbilical cord to the countryside is not cut. Whenever men build cities, they take the chance that their nurturing lifeline to the countryside may someday be severed, as indeed it was in wartime Poland. One of the most frightful images of the death of civilization envisages a time when the city, deprived of the countryside's surplus food and bloated by the countryside's surplus people, feeds upon its own ever-diminishing self and finally collapses. The starving inmates of Auschwitz, consuming their own substance until they wasted away into nothingness, may offer a prophetic image of urban civilization at the end of its journey from the countryside to Necropolis. Could it be that as the Jews were among the countryside's first exiles and among the pioneer inhabitants of Metropolis, so too they were among the first citizens of Necropolis, but that, unless current economic, social, and demographic trends are somehow reversed, there will be other citizens of the city of the dead, many others?

In conclusion, I would like to share with my readers some reflections on the political philosophy that undergirds this essay. This book is the result of one political conservative's attempt to reassess his views on politics and society in the aftermath of Watergate and the Nixon presidency. Hence, a word about political conservatism may be in order. Such a philosophy ought not to be equated with the defense of special privilege or the unrestricted acquisition of scarce resources by the few at the expense of the many. On the contrary, a genuine conservative would insist upon the responsibility of government to defend the public interest when it clearly conflicts with dominant private interests as well as impartially to reconcile the conflicting private interests within the body politic. It would also seem that a responsible conservative government would seek to mitigate rather than to exacerbate the worst inequities of condition and status within society. Such a government would not regard with unconcern the relentless growth of radical inequality in financial condition among its citizens. Furthermore, a genuine conservative government would defend the integrity of the political process and would recognize the difference between the political process and civil war. It is a very ancient tradition that in the political arena issues are to be decided by words and persuasion rather than by violence, bureaucratically administered terror, or the purchase of special advantage by either direct or indirect means.

Above all, a genuinely conservative government would seek to protect *every* citizen willing and able to work from the threat of economic redundancy. It is absurd to pretend that government has a responsibility to protect its citizens from theft and physical assault but has no responsibility to defend them from the infinitely greater violence perpetrated, often mindlessly, by institutions and policies that render millions of human beings literally useless. There is no private right or privilege that ought to be permitted to subvert the right of every person to a place of dignity and social utility within his or her community.

Much of this book has dealt with the fate of those who were rendered politically or economically redundant in the earlier decades of this century. Their story is one of the most terrible in the annals of the race. In a time of diminishing affluence and increasing mass unemployment, their story may carry a warning concerning our own future. *The history of the twentieth century has taught us that people who are rendered permanently superfluous are eventually condemned to segregated precincts of the living dead or are exterminated outright.* No genuine conservative could possibly defend policies or institutions that condemn an ever-multiplying number of people to such a fate. Such policies are recipes for unmitigated disaster. Before it is too late—and the hour is very late indeed—conservatives must distinguish themselves from defenders of selfish, anti-social privilege. They must also reflect upon the *revolutionary* and *destabilizing* impact of current rends in our economic system upon a growing number of our own population: Can any nation afford the unhindered functioning of a system that mindlessly produces an ever-enlarging pariah underclass of superfluous men and women who cannot be reached by the normal incentives and penalties of the established order? Lacking alternative means of controlling an underclass devoid of hope, is it realistic to expect that even a greatly enlarged police establishment, the state's instrument of violence against its own deviant citizens, will be able to contain the spreading social pathology such an underclass inevitably breeds? Is there not something profoundly wrong with a system in which political leaders look forward to a time when only five or six million members of the national work force will be condemned to permanent worklessness? Is there not a measure of madness in a system of technological rationality that first produces masses of surplus people and then holds forth extermination as the most "rational" and practical solution of the social problems they pose?

Notes

I wish to express my especial indebtedness to Raul Hilberg whose indispensable and magisterial work, *The Destruction of the European Jews*, contributed more to making this book possible than the work of any other scholar. Those acquainted with the literature on the Holocaust will recognize the extent of my indebtedness to Hilberg, a debt I acknowledge with much gratitude.

CHAPTER 1

1. Max Weber, "Politics as a Vocation," in *From Max Weber: Essays in Sociology*, trans. and ed. H. H. Gerth and C. Wright Mills (New York: Oxford University Press, 1946), p. 78.
2. See Raul Hilberg, *The Destruction of the European Jews* (Chicago: Quadrangle Books, 1967), pp. 31, 43 ff. Hilberg's book is the most comprehensive and balanced overview of the subject currently available. For a discussion of the role of bureaucracy in the definition of Jew and non-Jew in the Netherlands, see Jacob Presser, *The Destruction of the Dutch Jews*, trans. Arnold Pomerans (New York: Dutton, 1969), pp. 16 ff. For the text of "The First Ordinance to the Reich Citizenship Law," which was part of the so-called Nuremberg laws and which was the first German attempt legally to define a Jew (*Reichsgesetzblatt* [Reich Legal Gazette] 1935, I, 1333, enacted November 14, 1935), *see* Hilberg, *Documents of Destruction: Germany and Jewry* (Chicago: Quadrangle, 1971), pp. 18 ff.
3. Hilberg, *The Destruction*, pp. 31-39.
4. Ibid., p. 8.

5. The works on the roots of German anti-Semitism are exceedingly numerous. Among those of special relevance to the question of the origins of the death camps, see Hilberg, *The Destruction*, pp. 18ff.; Richard L. Rubenstein, *After Auschwitz* (Indianapolis: Bobbs-Merrill, 1966), pp. 1-44; Leon Poliakov, *Harvest of Hate* (Syracuse: Syracuse University Press, 1954); Jules Isaac, *The Teaching of Contempt: Christian Roots of Anti-Semitism*, trans. Helen Weaver (New York: Holt, Rhinehart and Winston, 1969; Rudolph M. Loewenstein, *Christians and Jews: A Psychoanalytic Study* (New York: International Universities Press, 1951); Malcolm Hay, *Europe and the Jews: The Pressure of Christendom on the People of Israel for 1900 Years* (Boston: Beacon Press, 1960); Franklin H. Littel, *The Crucifixion of the Jews* (New York: Harper & Row, 1974), pp. 24-43.

6. Gil Eliot, *Twentieth Century Book of the Dead* (New York: Scribner, 1972), pp. 41, 94, 124.

7. On Goebbels, see Louis P. Lochner, ed., *The Goebbels Diaries 1942-43* (Garden City, N.Y.: Doubleday, 1948), pp. 147-48; Roger Manvell and Heinrich Fraenkel, *Dr. Goebbels: His Life and Death* (New York: Simon and Schuster, 1960), pp. 195ff. On Himmler, see Gerald Reitlinger, *The SS, Alibi of a Nation* (New York: Putnam, 1968), p. 278. Reitlinger quotes extensively from Himmler's speech to SS officers in Posen, October 4, 1943 (Nuremberg Document PS-1918). See also Hilberg, *The Destruction*, p. 266; Roger Manvell and Heinrich Fraenkel, *Himmler* (New York: Putnam, 1965), pp. 131 ff.; Willi Frischauer, *Himmler: The Evil Genius of the Third Reich* (London: Odhams, 1953), pp. 148ff.

8. One of the most unfortunate legacies of the sixties has been the overly facile way in which terms such as *genocide* have been confused with the use of violence in wartime. As hideous as modern warfare may be, there is a difference between the use of even outrageous violence to compel the surrender of an enemy and the Nazi program of the systematic extermination of conquered peoples *after* they had surrendered.

9. Eliot, *Twentieth Century*, pp. 211-34.

10. Ibid., pp. 23, 218; see also *Encyclopedia Britannica*, (Chicago: 1962), s.v. "World War I."

11. For an account of Verdun, see Alistair Horne, *The Price of Glory: Verdun, 1916* (New York: Harper & Row, 1967), p. 36. Of particular interest is a memorandum by von Falkenhayn to the Kaiser written in December 1915 in which von Falkenhayn argues for a strategy by which "the forces of France will bleed to death." For a bitter account of the slaughter by a German soldier, see William Hermanns, *The Holocaust: From a Survivor of Verdun* (New York: Harper & Row, 1972), p. 1. Young Germans

marched off to war singing. *"Siegreich wollen wir Frankreich schlagen, sterben als ein tapferer* Held" (Victoriously we will crush France and die as brave heroes).

12. For a recent account of the Battle of the Somme, see Martin Middlebrook, *The First Day on the Somme* (New York: Norton, 1972). Middlebrook numbers the casualties of both sides as 1,300,000. He is less critical of Haig than many of Haig's other detractors. Those who defend Haig tend to assert that the British offensive at the Somme relieved pressure on the French at Verdun and thus made it possible for the French to remain in the war. See also Major-General Sir John Davidson, K.C.M.G., C.B., D.S.O., director of operations in France, 1916-1918, *Haig: Master of the Field* (London: P. Nevill, 1953) for a spirited defense of Haig. For Haig's own evaluation of the results, see *The Private Papers of Douglas Haig 1914-1918,* ed. Robert Blake (London: Eyre and Spottiswoode, 1952), p. 157. Although Haig could issue the orders that were to result in so many deaths, his son reports that "he felt it was his duty to refrain from visiting the casualty clearing stations because these visits made him physically ill." It was apparently easier to give impersonal commands than to confront their very human consequences. See *The Private Papers,* p. 9. One of Haig's most unremitting critics was Winston Churchill. See Churchill, *The World Crisis,* rev. ed. (London: Odhams, 1938), pp. 950-73, 1070-93. Haig was awarded the field marshall's baton on January 3, 1917 after the battle was over.

13. "In all biological populations there are innate devices to adjust population growth to the carrying capacity of the environment. Undoubtedly, some such device exists in man." Norman E. Borlaug, "The Green Revolution, Peace and Humility," Speech on accepting the Nobel Peace Prize, 1970, in *Population: A Clash of Prophets,* ed. Edward Pohlman (New York: New American Library, 1973), p. 241.

14. Order by Hitler, September 1, 1939, Nuremberg Document PS-710, cited by Hilberg, *The Destruction,* p. 561. See also Hannah Arendt, *The Origins of Totalitarianism* (New York: Harcourt Brace, 1951), pp. 45f. Nora Levin, *The Holocaust: The Destruction of European Jewry 1933-1945* (New York: Schocken, 1973), pp. 301-316. Helmut Krausnick and Martin Broszat, *Anatomy of the SS State,* trans. Dorothy Long and Marian Jackson (London: Paladin, 1968), pp. 112-13.

15. Lochner, *The Goebbels Diaries,* p. 148, and Arendt, *The Origins,* p. 349.

16. Lochner, *The Goebbels Diaries,* p. 29.

17. Eliot, *Twentieth Century,* p. 29.

18. For an informed discussion of the Turkish slaughter of the Armenians as a

distinctively modern exercise in mass violence, see Michael Arlen, "Passage to Arafat," *New Yorker*, February 3, 10, 17, 1975. Part 3 (February 17) is especially relevant.

19. Eliot, *Twentieth Century*, pp. 211 ff.
20. Maxim Gorky, *The Russian Peasant* (in Russian, Berlin: 1922), cited by Adam Ulam, *Lenin and the Bolsheviks: The Intellectual and Political History of the Triumph of Communism in Russia* (London: Fontana, 1969), p. 589.
21. Arendt, *The Origins*, p. 275. On the treaties, see Pablo De Azcarate, *League of Nations and National Minorities* (Washington: Carnegie Endowment for International Peace, 1945), and Oscar Janowsky, *The Jews and Minority Rights 1898-1919* (New York: Columbia University Press, 1933), pp. 321-390.
22. Arendt, *The Origins*, p. 275.
23. Arendt, Ibid., p. 279. See also Sir John F. Williams, "Denationalisation," in *British Year Book of International Law*, 1927. On statelessness and denaturalization, see John Hope Simpson, *The Refugee Problem* (Oxford: Oxford University Press, 1939).
24. The Spanish Republican army veterans were interned at camps at Argeles-sur-Mer and Cyprien. James G. MacDonald, *Encyclopedia Britannica* (Chicago: 1962), s.v. "Refugees."
25. See Martin Broszat, "The Concentration Camps 1933-45" in Krausnick and Broszat, *Anatomy of the SS State*, pp. 144 ff.
26. Eliot, *Twentieth Century*, pp. 187 ff.
27. The Evian conference (1938) on the refugee problem and the Bermuda conference (1943) are discussed by Arthur D. Morse, *While Six Million Died: A Chronicle of American Apathy* (New York: Random House, 1967), pp. 36-57, 163-80.
28. Alexander Weissberg, *Desperate Mission: Joel Brand's Story*, trans. Constantine FitzGibbon and Andrew Foster-Mellior (New York: Criterion, 1958), pp. 214-15.
29. This is the opinion of Hannah Arendt, *Eichmann in Jerusalem: A Report on the Banality of Evil* (New York: Viking, 1963), p. 77. At his trial in Jerusalem, Eichmann admitted that, in any event, extermination was the "final goal." See also Nora Levin, *The Holocaust*, p. 203 and Hilberg, *The Destruction*, pp. 258-61.
30. Ribbentrop to Hitler, December 9, 1938, "Documents on German Foreign Policy 1918-1945," Series D, vol. 4, *The Aftermath of Munich, 1938-39* (Washington: 1951), pp. 481 f., cited by Hilberg, p. 259.
31. Lochner, *The Goebbels Diaries*, p. 241. For a detailed description of the

policies of the Roosevelt administration with regard to the problem of the Jewish refugees, see Morse, *While Six Million Died*. For documents concerning British efforts to prevent the entry of Jewish refugees into Palestine, see Leni Yahil, "Select British Documents on the Illegal Immigration to Palestine (1939-1940)," *Yad Vashem Studies* (Jerusalem: 1974), 10: 241-76.

32. Al Carthill (Bennett Christian Huntington Calcraft Kennedy), *The Lost Dominion* (Edinburgh and London: W. Blackwood, 1924), pp. 93 ff. and Arendt, *The Origins*, pp. 210-12, 216, 221.

33. Hilberg, *The Destruction*, p. 771.

CHAPTER 2

1. Weber "Bureaucracy" in Gerth and Mills, *From Max Weber*, pp. 215-16.
2. Ibid., p. 214.
3. For Weber's discussion of his use of ideal types, see Weber, "Religious Rejections of the World and their Directions" in Gerth and Mills, *From Max Weber*, pp. 323-24. For a further discussion of Weber's use of ideal types, see Talcott Parsons, Introduction to Max Weber, *The Sociology of Religion*, trans. Ephraim Fischoff (Boston: Beacon, 1963), pp. lxv f. Reinhard Bendix, *Max Weber: An Intellectual Portrait*, (Garden City, N.Y.: Doubleday, 1960), pp. 278 ff. Julien Freund, *The Sociology of Max Weber*, trans. Mary Ilford (New York: Pantheon, 1970), pp. 59-71.
4. The root of Himmler's behavior is succinctly characterized by Manvell and Fraenkel, *Himmler*, p. 183: "Himmler was a man of violence, not by nature, but by conviction." For a description of Himmler's reaction to actual killing, see Hilberg, *The Destruction*, pp. 218 f.
5. Perhaps the best known example of this is Himmler's speech to SS officers in Posen, October 4, 1943 (Nuremberg Document PS-1918). The speech is printed in *Nazi Conspiracy and Aggression*, 10 vols. (Washington: 1946-48), 4: 558-78. The theme of overcoming the difficulty involved in the work of extermination is also expressed by Himmler in his May, 1944 speech to the Nazi Gauleiters; *see* Manvell and Fraenkel, *The Incomparable Crime* (New York: Putnam, 1967), pp. 43 f.
6. Broszat, "The Concentration Camps" in Krausnick and Broszat, *Anatomy*, pp. 165 ff.
7. Ibid., pp. 165 ff.
8. Ibid., p. 179.

9. Arendt, *The Origins*, p. 449.

10. Hilberg, *The Destruction*, p. 235; see also pp. 101 ff.

11. Helmut Krausnick, "The Persecution of the Jews" in Krausnick and Broszat, *Anatomy*, pp. 57 ff.; Hilberg, *The Destruction*, pp. 23-30. The view that Goebbels was the instigator is not universally held. Nora Levin places the responsibility on Heydrich in *The Holocaust*, pp. 80 ff. Albert Speer, however, insists that Goebbels was responsible: See Albert Speer, *Inside the Third Reich*, trans. Richard and Clara Winston (New York: Macmillan, 1970), p. 112.

12. Hilberg, *The Destruction*, pp. 23-30.

13. *Ibid.*

14. *Ibid.*

15. Nuremberg Document NG-1672, cited by Hilberg, *The Destruction*, p. 29.

16. Peter Berger, *The Sacred Canopy* (Garden City, N.Y.: Doubleday, 1967), p. 107.

17. Max Weber, "Science as a Vocation" in Gerth and Mills, *From Max Weber*, p. 139.

18. Max Weber, "The Sociology of the World Religions" in Gerth and Mills, *From Max Weber*, p. 293.

19. Berger, *Sacred Canopy*, pp. 99, 116, 118.

20. The thesis that the "systematic rationalization of means and ends in the spheres of conduct and belief" is in large measure a consequence of the cultural ethos engendered by that form of Protestantism known as Puritanism, especially Calvinism, is, of course, Weber's. For an informed and sophisticated defense of the Weber thesis, see Benjamin Nelson, "Weber's Protestant Ethic: Its Origins, Wanderings, and Foreseeable Future" in *Beyond the Classics? Essays in the Scientific Study of Religion*, ed. Charles Y. Glock and Phillip E. Hammond (New York: Harper and Row, 1973), pp. 70-130. For a discussion of the central importance of the biblical doctrine of a supramundane God for the development of rational capitalism in Weber's thought, see David Little, *Religion, Order and Law: A Study in Pre-Revolutionary England* (New York: Harper and Row, 1969), pp. 6–32.

21. Berger, *Sacred Canopy*, p. 121.

22. Ibid., p. 124.

23. Fundamental to the view presented here is the paradoxical conviction that *it has been the destiny of biblical religion to negate itself in ever-widening domains of human activity.* The observations of Karl Löwith are especially

relevant: "Philosophical criticism of the Christian religion began in the nineteenth century with Hegel and reached its climax with Nietzsche. *It is a Protestant movement,* and therefore specifically German . . . *Our critical philosophers were all theologically educated Protestants, and their criticism of Christianity presupposes its Protestant manifestations.*" (Italics added) According to Löwith, Hegel "translates" the forms of religion, which belong properly speaking to the imagination, into the conceptualization of reason, but "the historical consequence of Hegel's ambiguous 'translation' was *an absolute destruction of Christian philosophy and of the Christian religion.*" The important point in Löwith's analysis for our purposes is that Hegel's "destruction" takes place *within the Protestant tradition* and is the spiritual work of an *insider.* See Karl Löwith, *From Hegel to Nietzsche: The Revolution in Nineteenth-Century Thought,* trans. David E. Green (New York: Holt, Rhinehart and Winston, 1964), pp. 327-33. See also Löwith, "The Historical Background of European Nihilism" and "Hegel and the Christian Religion" in Karl Löwith, *Nature, History and Existentialism and Other Essays in the Philosophy of Religion,* ed. Arnold Levison (Evanston: Northwestern University Press, 1966), pp. 10 f., 162-203.

According to Alexander Kojève, Hegel maintained that the realization of the true content of Christianity is radical atheism and human autonomy devoid of any opposing transcendence. See Alexandre Kojève, *Introduction to the Reading of Hegel: Lectures on the Phenomenology of the Spirit,* ed. Allan Bloom, trans. James H. Nichols, Jr., (New York: Basic Books, 1969), pp. 66-70. Hegel thus saw the secularization process as a dialectical consequence of Christianity long before contemporary sociologists of religion made the same point in their discipline. See Thomas Luckmann, *The Invisible Religion* (New York: Macmillan, 1967), pp. 22 ff. and John Murray Cuddihy, *The Ordeal of Civility: Freud, Marx, Levi-Strauss, and the Jewish Struggle with Modernity,* (New York: Basic Books, 1974), pp. 3-12, 225-38. The Christian roots of radical secularity have been given theological expression in the writings of Thomas J. J. Altizer; see especially Thomas J. J. Altizer, *The Descent into Hell: A Study of the Radical Reversal of the Christian Consciousness* (Philadelphia: Lippincott, 1970).

24. This is the view of Emil L. Fackenheim. See Emil Fackenheim, *Encounters Between Judaism and Modern Philosophy: A Preface to Future Jewish Thought* (New York: Basic Books, 1973), pp. 157, 192-95. For a rejoinder, see Richard L. Rubenstein, "The Radical Monotheism of Emil Fackenheim" *Soundings,* Summer, 1974.

25. An enumeration of the denaturalization decrees is to be found in John Hope Simpson, *The Refugee Problem,* pp. 231-39.

26. The cancellation of naturalizations was enacted on July 14, 1933. The provision for the cancellation of citizenship of those residing abroad was enacted on July 26, 1933. See Simpson, *The Refugee Problem*, p. 234.
27. Hilberg, *The Destruction*, p. 301.
28. Thierack to Bormann, Nuremberg Document, NG-558, cited by Hilberg, *The Destruction*, p. 296.

CHAPTER 3

1. *See* David Brion Davis, *The Problem of Slavery in Western Culture* (Ithaca, N.Y.: Cornell University Press, 1966), p. 273.
2. Stanley M. Elkins, *Slavery: A Problem in American Institutional and Intellectual Life* (Chicago: University of Chicago Press, 1959) and Frank Tannenbaum, *Slaves and Citizen: The Negro in the Americas* (New York: Knopf, 1947).
3. Elkins, *Slavery*, pp. 68-71, 73f.
4. Ibid., pp. 65–67
5. The tendency of hierocratic orders to develop a non-rational economic ethic and to oppose other centers of power fostering a rational ethic (e. g. the bourgeoisie) is discussed by Max Weber, *Economy and Society: An Outline of Interpretive Sociology*, ed. Guenther Roth and Claus Wittich (New York: Bedminster, 1968), 3: 1185 ff. On the political and social impotence of the antebellum Southern church, see Elkins, *Slavery*, p. 61.
6. Elkins, *Slavery*, pp. 52-80.
7. Davis, *The Problem of Slavery*, pp. 253 ff. The scholarly responses to the Elkins' thesis have shown how difficult it is to generalize about the differences between slavery in North and South America or, for that matter, within either continent. See Sidney W. Mintz, "Review of Stanley M. Elkins' *Slavery*," *American Anthropologist*, LXIII, June 1961, pp. 579-87; Arnold Sio, "The Slave Status in the Americas" in *Slavery in the New World*, ed. Laura Foner and Eugene D. Genovese (Englewood Cliffs, N.J.: Prentice-Hall, 1969), pp. 96-112; Eugene D. Genovese, "The Treatment of Slaves in Different Countries: Problems in the Application of the Comparative Method" in Foner and Genovese, op. cit., pp. 202-10; Eugene D. Genovese, "Materialism and Idealism in the History of Negro Slavery in the Americas" in Foner and Genovese, op. cit., pp. 238-55.
8. Thus, when it was more economical to work slaves to death than to keep them in good health, as was the case in the mines of Brazil and some of the plantations of the West Indies, "there was little incentive to improve conditions or limit hours of work." Davis, *The Problem of Slavery*, p. 258.

9. Davis, *The Problem of Slavery*, pp. 282 ff; see also Elkins, *Slavery*, p. 57.

10. Elkins, *Slavery*, pp. 98-139.

11. Davis, *The Problem of Slavery*, p. 23; see Tannenbaum, *Slave and Citizen*, pp. 31 f.

12. Eugene D. Genovese, *Roll, Jordan, Roll: The World the Slaves Made* (New York: Pantheon, 1974), p. 57.

13. "The slaves, by accepting a paternalistic class rule, developed their most powerful defense against the dehumanization implicit in slavery." Eugene D. Genovese, *Roll, Jordan, Roll*, p. 7, see pp. 3-7; see also Eugene D. Genovese, *The World the Slaveholders Made* (New York: Pantheon, 1969), pp. 98 f. for a discussion of factors making for the humane treatment of the slaves in the South. The same topic is discussed by Genovese in greater detail in *Roll, Jordan, Roll*, especially pp. 49-75.

14. Genovese, *Roll, Jordan, Roll*, pp. 41 f.

15. Jürgen Kuczynski quotes Senator Martin Griffin of Massachusetts in a report to the U.S. Senate Judiciary Committee dated April 29, 1865: "The result of the prosperity of which we boast . . . has a tendency to make the working man little else than a machine. . . . in the language of one of the witnesses, 'than a slave: for,' he added, 'we are slaves; overworked, worn out and enfeebled by toil; with no time left for improvement of mind or soul." Jürgen Kuczynski, *The Rise of the Working Class*, trans. C.T.A. Roy (New York: McGraw-Hill, 1967), p. 181.

16. Kuczynski, *Working Class*, p. 181.

17. Hilberg, *The Destruction*, pp. 332-45.

18. Davis, *The Problem of Slavery*, p. 76.

18a. The classic description of working class life in England in the 1840s is, of course, Friedrich Engels, *The Condition of the Working-Class in England* (1845) (Moscow: Progess Publishers, 1973). Engels' work offers a glimpse of the hell created by the industrial revolution. The anal character of the hell was graphically described by Engels long before Freud and Norman O. Brown. Stephen Marcus has written about England's urban poor of the period: "millions of English men and women were virtually living in shit. . . . Thus generations of human beings, out of whose lives the wealth of England was produced, were compelled to live in wealth's symbolic, negative counterpart." Stephen Marcus, *Engels, Manchester and the Working Class* (New York: Random House, 1974), pp. 184 f. See Eric Hobsbawn, *The Age of Revolution* (Cleveland: World, 1962), pp. 205-8; for a discussion of the degraded condition of England's agricultural workers at the inception of the industrial revolution, see Eric Hobsawn and George Rude, *Captain Swing* (New York: Pantheon, 1968), pp. 51 ff.

19. It is difficult to calculate the loss in lives exacted by the slave trade. "All figures are estimates, but it has been said that about one third of the Negroes taken from their homes died on the way to the coast and at embarkation stations, and that another third died crossing the ocean and in the seasoning, so that only one third finally survived to become the laborers and colonizers of the New World." Frank Tennenbaum, *Slaves and Citizens*, pp. 28 f.; see Elkins, *Slavery*, pp. 98 ff.

20. Davis, *The Problem of Slavery*, p. 258.

21. Eugene D. Genovese, *The Political Economy of Slavery: Studies in the Economy and Society of the Slave South* (New York: Pantheon, 1961), pp. 243-74, especially p. 247.

22. Tannenbaum, *Slaves and Citizens*, pp. 65-71, 104-10; Davis, *The Problem of Slavery*, pp. 70-74, 289-301.

23. "The colored slave woman became the medium through which two great races were united." W.E.B. Du Bois, *The Gift of the Black Folk: The Negroes in the Making of America* (Boston: The Stratford Company, 1924), p. 146. Cited by Genovese in his discussion of miscegenation in *Roll, Jordan, Roll*, pp. 413-31; see Kenneth M. Stampp, *The Peculiar Institution: Slavery in the Ante-Bellum South* (New York: Knopf, 1956), pp. 350-61.

24. Hilberg, *The Destruction*, p. 578.

25. Ibid., p. 249.

26. Ibid., pp. 177-256

27. Hilberg, *The Destruction*, pp. 218 f., 565 ff. Reitlinger, *The SS: Alibi of A Nation 1922-1945*, pp. 281-88

28. Hilberg, *The Destruction*, pp. 556 ff.

CHAPTER 4

1. Hilberg, *The Destruction*, p. 603.

2. Ibid., p. 608.

3. Hilberg, *The Destruction*, p. 608; see Manvell and Fraenkel *Himmler*, pp. 50, 111-12 and Frischauer, *Himmler*, pp. 95-97.

4. "Partly Jewish is anyone who is descended from one or two grandparents who are fully Jewish by race. . . . A grandparent is to be considered as fully Jewish if he belonged to the Jewish religious community." Article 2 of the First Ordinance to the Reich Citizenship Law, November 14, 1935, *Reichsgesetzblatt* 1935, I, 1333, in Hilberg, *Documents of Destruction*, pp. 19f.

5. Hilberg, *The Destruction*, p. 273.

6. Frischauer, *Himmler*, pp. 183 f.
7. Frischauer, *Himmler*, p. 184; Hilberg, *The Destruction*, pp. 605 f. When Clauberg returned to Germany in 1951 after having been a prisoner of war in Russia, he told reporters that he had finally perfected a simplified method of sterilization and that he was looking forward to its application in "special cases". "Nazi Camp Doctor Back In Germany", *New York Times*, October 18, 1955, p. 10. Cited by Hilberg, *The Destruction*, p. 609.
8. Frischauer, *Himmler*, p. 184; Hilberg, *The Destruction*, p. 606.
9. Hilberg, *The Destruction*, p. 607.
10. Jessica Mitford, *Kind and Usual Treatment: The Prison Business* (New York: Knopf, 1973), pp. 138-68. On the syphilis experiments, see S. Hiltner, "Tuskegee Syphilis Study Under Review," *Christian Century*, Nov. 28, 1973; J. Slater, "Condemned to Die for Science: Tuskegee Study," *Ebony*, Nov. 1972; "Convicts as Guinea Pigs," *Time*, March 19, 1973. On the question of the use and abuse of prisoners for drug company sponsored experiments, see also "Experiments Behind Bars: Doctors, Drug Companies and Prisoners", *Atlantic*, May 1973; Carl Rogers, "Clockwork Orange in California," *Christian Century*, October 31, 1973.
11. Stampp, *The Peculiar Institution*, pp. 8-9; Elkins, *Slavery*, p. 61. Genovese sees the racism of the slaveholders as a rationalization of their policies rather than as a cause. Genovese, *Roll, Jordan, Roll*, p. 58.
12. "A Well Meaning Act," *Newsweek*, July 16, 1973, pp. 26-31; Richard F. Babcock, Jr., "Sterilization: Coercing Consent," *Nation*, January 12, 1974. In 1971 seventeen states had laws providing for compulsory sterilization. "Sterilization: Newest Threat to the Poor," *Ebony*, October, 1973, pp. 150 ff.
13. Hilberg, *The Destruction*, pp. 601 f.
14. Karl Marx and Friedrich Engels, "Manifesto of the Communist Party" in Marx and Engels, *Basic Writings on Politics and Philosophy* ed. Lewis S. Feuer (Garden City, N.Y.: Anchor, 1959), p. 9.
15. Weber, "Bureaucracy" in Gerth and Mills, *From Max Weber*, p. 223.
16. Marx and Engels, "Manifesto" in *Basic Writings*, p. 14.
17. Ibid.
18. See Arthur Redford and W.H. Chaloner, *Labour Migration in England 1800-1850* (Manchester: Manchester University Press, 1964) (First edition: 1924). Kuczynski, *Working Class*, pp. 140-84; Hobsbawm, *The Age of the Revolution*, pp. 200-208.
19. For Marx, workers are not only "slaves" of the "bourgeois class" and the "bourgeois state", but of the very machines they themselves have pro-

duced. Thus the workers are enslaved by their own product. See Marx and Engels "Manifesto" in *Basic Writings*, p. 14. "The dominion of 'dead' objectified labour over living labour steadily increases. Machinery thus magnifies alienation." Shlomo Avineri, *The Social and Political Thought of Karl Marx* (Cambridge: Cambridge University Press, 1968), p. 121.

20. "The labour movement was an organization of self-defence, of protest, of revolution. But for the labouring poor it was more than a tool of struggle: it was also a way of life." Hobsbawm, *The Age of Revolution*, p. 214.

21. On von Weinberg, see Hilberg, *The Destruction*, pp. 58 f.

22. Hilberg, *The Destruction*, pp. 592f.

23. Hilberg, *The Destruction*, p. 751 n. Perhaps the technocratic attitude towards slave labor was best expressed by an observation of Albert Speer: "my obsessional fixation on production and output statistics blurred all considerations and feelings of humanity. An American historian has said of me that I loved machines more than people. He is not wrong. . . . the sight of suffering people influenced only my emotions, but not my conduct. On the plane of feelings only sentimentality emerged; in the realm of decisions on the other hand, I continued to be ruled by the principles of utility." Albert Speer, *Inside the Third Reich*, p. 375.

24. Hilberg, *The Destruction*, p. 595 f.

25. Ibid.

26. Ibid., p. 596.

27. For the dreary story of corporate disloyalty, see George W. Stocking and Myron W. Watkins, *Cartels in Action: Studies in International Business Diplomacy* (New York: The Twentieth Century Fund, 1946), pp. 466-518; Guenter Reimann, *Patents for Hitler* (New York: Vanguard, 1942); Richard Sasuly, *I.G. Farben*, (New York: Boni and Gaer, 1947). I am indebted to Dr. Irving Sobel and Dr. Jacob Simmons of the Department of Economics at Florida State University for their assistance in coming to understand I.G. Farben's cartel arrangements with American corporations both before and during World War II.

28. Sasuly, *I.G. Farben*, p. 126.

29. Hilberg, *The Destruction*, pp. 595 f.

30. Ibid., pp. 567-572.

31. Ibid., p. 571.

32. Ibid., p. 567 f.

33. Ibid., pp. 704-15. Hilberg has a very instructive list of the leading participants in the extermination project and what happened to them after the war.

34. Adam Ulam, *Lenin and the Bolsheviks*, p. 583.
35. "Germanys Condemn U.S. On Executions," *New York Times*, June 8, 1951, p. 5.

CHAPTER 5

1. Quoted by Hilberg, *The Destruction*, p. 529.
2. Ibid., pp. 529 f.; Levin, *The Holocaust*, pp. 612 ff.; Randolph L. Braham, "What Did They Know and When?" Working paper presented at International Scholars Conference on the Holocaust—One Generation After sponsored by the Hebrew University, Jerusalem, New York, March 2-6, 1975; *Hungarian-Jewish Studies*, ed. Randolph L. Braham (New York: World Federation of Hungarian Jews, 1966); Eugene Levai, *Black Book on the Martyrdom of Hungarian Jewry* (Zurich and Vienna: 1948)
3. Levai, *Black Book*, p. 134.
4. Jacob Neusner, *From Politics to Piety: The Emergence of Pharisaic Judaism* (Englewood Heights, N.J.: 1973), p. 148.
5. Hilberg, *The Destruction*, p. 16.
6. Ibid., pp. 122 ff.
7. Weber, "Bureaucracy" in Gerth and Mills, *From Max Weber*, p. 197.
8. See Hannah Arendt, *Eichmann in Jerusalem: A Report on the Banality of Evil*, p. 90.
9. For a detailed discussion of the responses of the various Jewish councils to German "resettlement" programs, see Isaiah Trunk, *Judenrat: The Jewish Councils in Eastern Europe Under Nazi Occupation* (New York: Macmillan, 1972), pp. 388-474. For the response of the Dutch Jewish Council, see Jacob Presser, *The Destruction of the Dutch Jews*, pp. 238-77.
10. Leo Baeck in *We Survived*, ed. Eric H. Boehm, 2nd ed. (Santa Barbara, Cal.: Clio Press, 1966), p. 290.
11. The *public* debate over the roll of the *Judenräte* in collaborating with the Nazis began with the publication of Hannah Arendt's *Eichmann in Jerusalem* which appeared in *The New Yorker* in February and March 1963. However, the fundamental issues had already been stated with magisterial authority by Raul Hilberg in *The Destruction* in 1961. For a response to Dr. Arendt, see Jacob Robinson, *And the Crooked Shall be Made Straight* (Philadelphia: Jewish Publication Society, 1965). Isaiah Trunk's *Judenrat* is the most comprehensive discussion of the roll of the *Judenräte*. However, neither Trunk's book nor his own research have caused Hilberg to alter his

opinion that the councils were fundamentally instruments of Jewish self-destruction. See Hilberg, "The Ghetto as a Form of Government: An Analysis of Isaiah Trunk's *Judenrat,*" paper presented at the International Scholars Conference on the Holocaust—One Generation After, New York, March 2-6, 1975. For a response to Hilberg's current position on the Jewish Councils, see Yehuda Bauer, "Jewish Leadership Reactions to Nazi Policies," paper presented at International Scholars Conference.
12. Emanuel Ringelblum, *Notes from the Warsaw Ghetto* (New York: McGraw-Hill, 1958), p. 310.
13. Trunk, *Judenrat,* p. 552; Hilberg, *The Destruction,* p. 322.
14. Weber, "Bureaucracy" in Gerth and Mills, *From Max Weber,* p. 229.

CHAPTER 6

1. Ulam, *Lenin and the Bolsheviks,* pp. 622-24.
2. *See* Adam Ulam, *Stalin: The Man and His Era* (New York: Viking, 1973), pp. 322-56.
3. I wrote this sentence in August 1974. Since then there has been much evidence that the I.R.S. and other federal agencies were far less independent of the executive than I then believed. There is no doubt that it was Nixon's objective to eliminate all such independence. I have let the sentence stand because Nixon did not wholly succeed before his forcible removal from office. The danger, of course, remains. For a chilling account of the misuse of the federal bureaucracy to harass the communications media, see Thomas Whiteside, "Annals of Television: Shaking the Tree" in *New Yorker,* March 17, 1975, pp. 75 ff.
4. For an overview of the current debate concerning voluntary vs. imposed policies to limit family size and ultimately to reduce population trends, see *Population: A Clash of Prophets,* ed. Edward Pohlman, pp. 295-435. Wayne Bartz proposes that the state impose punitive measures upon all parents "guilty" of having more than two offspring. See Wayne Bartz, "Outrageous Solutions to the Population Outrage," in Pohlman, *Population,* p. 297. However, an examination of the other selections included by Pohlman reveals that many population experts find nothing "outrageous" in Bartz' "outrageous proposal." The earliest "outrageous proposal" of the sort that achieved general currency was Jonathan Swift's proposal that "a young healthy child, well nursed, is at a Year old, a most delicious, nourishing, and wholesome Food; whether Stewed, Roasted, Baked or Boiled.

. . ." Such was Dean Swift's "solution" to the twin problems of food shortage and population surplus in Ireland. Jonathan Swift, *A Modest Proposal for Preventing the Children of Poor People in Ireland from Being a Burden to Their Parents or Country, and for Making Them Beneficial to the Publick* in *Prose Works of Jonathan Swift*, ed. H. Davis (Oxford: Oxford University Press, 1955), 12: 109-18.

5. *See* David Bakan, *Slaughter of the Innocents: A Study of the Battered Child Phenomenon* (Boston: Beacon, 1972), pp. 78-106.

6. Arendt, *Origins*, p. 431.

7. According to Sidney M. Willhelm, a black sociologist, genocide may be the fate awaiting America's unemployable minorities. His analysis deserves more attention than it has received. See Sidney M. Willhelm, *Who Needs the Negro?* (Garden City, N.Y.: Anchor, 1971).

8. Hilberg, *The Destruction*, p. 687.

9. For a discussion of reactions to the War Crimes trials by American policy makers, theologians and social scientists, see William J. Bosch, *Judgement on Nuremberg: American Attitudes Toward the Major German War-Crimes Trials* (Chapel Hill, N.C.: University of North Carolina Press, 1970).

10. "The disinterested tendency to inflict punishment is a distinctive characteristic of the lower middle class, that is, of a social class living under conditions which force its members to an extraordinarily high degree of self restraint and subject them to much frustration of natural desires." This is the conclusion of Sven Ranulf in his study of the rise of institutions for the disinterested infliction of punishment in the western world and the abandonment of earlier resort to private or clan revenge. Sven Ranulf, *Moral Indignation and Middle Class Psychology* (New York: Schocken, 1964), p. 198. For an overview of biblical attitudes toward private revenge and public punishment, see Roland de Vaux, *Ancient Israel*, (New York: McGraw-Hill, 1966), 1: 158-63.

11. For another view, see Gideon Hausner, *Justice in Jerusalem*, (New York: Schocken, 1974).

12. The arguments were usually framed in the form of Social Darwinist ideology. See Hans-Gunter Zmärlik, "Social Darwinism in Germany, Seen as an Historical Problem" in *Republic into Reich: The Making of the Nazi Revolution*, ed. Hajo Holborn (New York: Pantheon, 1972), pp. 435-74. See Geoffrey Barraclough, "Farewell to Hitler" in *New York Review of Books*, April 3, 1975.

13. Rubenstein, *After Auschwitz*.

14. Sigmund Freud, *Totem and Taboo*, trans. James Strachey (New York: Norton, 1962, 1913).

15. G.W.F. Hegel, *The Phenomenology of the Mind*, trans. J.B. Baillie (London: George Allen and Unwin, 1931), pp. 229-40. See also Alexandre Kojève, *Introduction to the Reading of Hegel*, pp. 3-30 and Jean Hyppolyte, *Genesis and Structure of Hegel's Phenomenology of Spirit*, trans. Samuel Cherniak and John Heckman (Evanston: Northwestern University Press, 1974), pp. 156-77.